D0606674

THE
COUNTRY FAIR
COOKBOOK

by

ALISON BOTELER

BARRON'S

Many thanks to my father and Jackee for helping to
make this book possible

Copyright © 1995 by Alison Boteler

All rights reserved. No part of this book may be reproduced in
any form, by photostat, microfilm, xerography, or any other
means, or incorporated into any information retrieval system,
electronic or mechanical, without the written permission of
the copyright owner.

All inquiries should be addressed to:
Barron's Educational Series, Inc.
250 Wireless Boulevard
Hauppauge, New York 11788-3917

Library of Congress Catalog Card No. 94-42420

ISBN 0-8120-6522-0

Library of Congress Cataloging-in-Publication Data
Boteler, Alison Molinare.
    The country fair cookbook / by Alison Boteler.
      p.   cm.
    ISBN 0-8120-6522-0
    1. Cookery, American 2. Baking—United States I. Title.
TX715.B667 1994
641.5973—dc20   94-42420
                   CIP

PRINTED IN HONG KONG
567   9927   987654321

THE COUNTRY FAIR COOKBOOK

❖

INTRODUCTION

❖

This is a book about traditions, not trends. Every few years someone tries to reinvent American food. Fortunately our favorite dishes have managed to survive fleeting fads. Classic American cooking is alive and well—and is being dished out at country fairs. All across the nation, these events are bigger than ever before. The same excitement that drew people a century ago draws them today. Before there were theme parks, there were country fairs complete with Ferris wheels and carnival rides. For some, they were a chance to sample the best of everything, from fried chicken to towering lemon meringue pies. For others, it was a chance to compete . . . with the hope of bringing home a blue ribbon for perfect bread-and-butter pickles.

Every region is steeped in its own culture, and food festivals share these local flavors with everyone. Pig roasts and lobster fests are one big party with an open invitation to all. Firehouse barbecues and church chili suppers unite small towns and suburban communities in social gatherings. Holiday bazaars challenge bakers' imaginations and talents, helping to fund the charities that fuel our nation. They are all spin-offs of the country fair spirit . . . a celebration of real American food the way most of us remember it and treasure it.

❖   ❖   ❖   ❖

COUNTRY COOKING NOTES

❖

Through the years, I've been a patron of, participant in, and even judge at many country fairs, food festivals, and holiday bazaars. When it comes to country cooking, certain tips, techniques, and truisms are commonly shared. Wherever possible, I've sown the seeds of that wisdom throughout this book. In addition, I hope you'll find these "country cooking notes" a helpful reference.

❖

BUTTER AND SHORTENING

*The distinctive flavor of traditional country baked goods comes from a critical ingredient: farm-fresh, sweet cream butter. Most of us do not have cows in the backyard or butter churns in the kitchen. We have to make do with what's commercially available at the supermarket. That's why all of the recipes in this book that call for butter specify **unsalted** butter. It's the closest thing in taste to churned butter; it brings out the best in food. You might see salt in the recipe and wonder, "Why bother using unsalted butter if I'm going to add salt?" For one thing, unsalted butter has a lower moisture content than the salted kind—so you're getting more butter and less water, ounce for ounce. Then too, salt acts as a preservative, so when you buy salted butter, you're often getting a product that's been on the shelf a while. Unsalted butter has a fresher, sweeter, "butterier" flavor. It always makes a difference in the end, and the end result is what your effort's all about.*

*What about that other stuff? Well, margarine just flies in the face of country baking. Your cookies and cakes will taste as though they came from the corner deli. It's even more crucial that diet margarine and butter blends **never** be substituted for the real thing. These sticks and spreads have a very high water content and are held together with gelatin, stabilizers, or rice flour. They break down when heated, and result in baking disasters.*

Alas, there are times when even the moisture content of old-fashioned butter is too high for certain baked goods to achieve the proper texture. These recipes once called for lard; today they generally use shortening. (Even I wouldn't expect anyone to bake with lard in this day and age!) But let's be frank . . . shortening is blah; its flavor a cut above cold cream. Many prizewinning bakers have worked around this dilemma by using butter-flavored shortening. It's a practical product when used correctly: as a substitute for shortening, not butter.

❖

BROWN SUGAR

Brown sugar is white sugar flavored with molasses. It's the essence of American, as opposed to European, baking. Much of the character we've come to expect in nostalgic desserts relies on brown sugar. But there's a difference in brown sugars; whether to use light or dark depends on the recipe. Throughout this book, ingredients always specify "light brown sugar" or "dark brown sugar."

❖

NUTS

Pecans, walnuts, and almonds cannot be appreciated until they've been toasted. Once you've tasted the difference that toasting makes, you'll never use "green" nuts again—it's like comparing pralines to plywood. A memo on how to toast nuts appears with every recipe calling for them.

❖

ROLLING IN DOUGH

If you don't have a fancy marble counter, don't despair. Nothing beats a floured pastry cloth with a rolling pin cover (stocking): it reduces, and sometimes eliminates, the need for prechilling dough. I've never been satisfied with butcher block (or marble for that matter) because dough sticks to the rolling pin regardless of the surface. The floured cloth and stocking virtually eliminates this problem. It's also flexible, so you can lift and turn the cloth as you work with your dough. This allows you to easily fold up a circle of pie pastry and slip it into a pan.

MIXING METHODS

An electric mixer is indispensable for certain baked goods—whipping meringue by hand would wear out your arm. Years ago, cake batters were made by adding liquid and dry ingredients alternately. Thanks to modern mixers, many traditional recipes are now easily converted to the one-bowl beating method. But mixer speeds and minutes must be monitored like a rocket launch; overbeating or underbeating can destroy the texture of your cake.

Which brings me to another subject . . . **never** *use an electric mixer for muffins or any other recipe that calls for blending ingredients by hand. You'll develop the gluten in the flour and end up with hockey pucks! However, developing the gluten in bread is important; that's what kneading is all about. If the thought of kneading makes you tired, then you need to use a dough hook attachment on your mixer.*

Finally, I'd like to say a word about wire whisks. Can anyone live without them? We tend to think of them as a French gadget, but my great-grandmother had one that seemed prehistoric. True, it didn't look like the balloon whisks of today, but it served its purpose. Whisking is the only way to ensure smooth sauces, gravies, and custards. It's also a useful tool for blending dry ingredients—flour, leavening, sugar, and spices.

BAKING PANS AND PARCHMENT

Always use heavy-duty, nonreflective baking sheets for cookies, biscuits, and breads. Thin, shiny pans will inevitably burn the bottoms of your baked goods. The same goes for cake pans. (If you're using glass cake pans, reduce the oven temperature by about 25°F.)

Sometimes I'll still grease and flour a cake pan, but I honestly couldn't live without **baking parchment.** *This paper enables cakes to effortlessly flip out of pans after they've cooled. It takes the heartache out of making (and breaking) batch after batch of cookies. Every cookie recipe in this book is baked on parchment paper because I strongly believe it's the difference between success and frustration.*

When baking pies, place them on the next to lowest oven rack, on a heavy baking sheet. (Cover the sheet with aluminum foil to protect it from spills or "volcanic" fruit filling eruptions.) This method ensures that the bottom crust will brown.

When baking quick breads, grease the **bottoms** only of loaf pans. These batters need to climb up the sides of the pan. I often use disposable foil gift pans with lids. These are great for bringing nut breads or fruitcakes to holiday bazaars; they never have to leave the pan.

❖

MASON JARS AND JELLY JARS

The lost art of pickling and preserving is still alive and well at country fairs. To do it properly you must have the proper tools. You need a large kettle for sterilizing jars and for water-bath processing. Tongs with a good firm grip are essential for handling jars. There are two types of mason jars to choose from: those with two-piece lids or those with glass lids that clamp on (I find these awkward to work with, and rarely use them). I never use anything larger than a pint jar. It's simply too difficult to handle a quart jar in the water bath; they get quite heavy and slip out of the tongs. Half-pint jelly jars also come with two-piece lids. I can't emphasize enough the importance of labeling jams, jellies, and conserves. You may think you know what it is now—but what about six months from now? Ten batches later, it's hard to tell the cherries from the cranberries. I once judged a jelly contest in which the specimens were really jumbled up—the apple butter was switched with the pear spread, and the apricot preserves were confused with the peaches.

❖

TAKING IT WITH YOU

If you're bringing any kind of baked goods to a bazaar, remember your climate. Humidity makes meringue pies weep and cookies soggy. Take these conditions into consideration before choosing a recipe, and then do your best to transport it properly. Store items that are meant to stay crisp in tightly sealed containers, before they're exposed to the air. Likewise, you don't want to allow moist cakes and bar cookies to dry out. The same containers that keep moisture out will also keep it in. Over the years, I've *collected stackable pie containers and portable cake safes tall enough for a layer cake or a high meringue pie. Look for these in the housewares department of discount stores.*

Some things are simply better when baked at the last possible minute; fruit pies are a prime example. Other foods are better when prepared a day ahead: vegetable salads that need to marinate improve overnight. Potato salad and mayonnaise-type dressings need a reasonable amount of time to develop flavor, but not too long.

Every possible precaution should be used to prevent chilled dishes from spoiling. Food poisoning is a potential hazard at any public gathering. Use an insulated ice chest and frozen thermal blocks until you can get to on-site refrigeration.

Finally, don't lose your supplies! It's amazing how everyone's stuff can get mixed up. Label your containers and pans. (I learned the hard way that half of your kitchen can be spread around town. I'm still using a strange roasting pan for my Thanksgiving turkey.) Chili suppers are notorious for this problem—everyone shows up with similar things, which then pile up on counters and sinks. No one wants to tackle the dishes until it's too late, and the original owners have gone home. Solution: Transfer as much food as possible into disposable containers before entering a community kitchen. It will make cleanup easier for everyone.

COUNTRY FAIR FAVORITES

❖

Bake-offs and bake sale tables will always be a major focal point of state or country fairs. In times past, small wars have started over the "perfect pie." A panel of impartial judges had to be carefully selected. At many events, blindfolded taste testing is still practiced to this day. The competition is tough, and so is the scrutiny: from blowing on piecrust to cutting cakes with a feather. Texture and appearance are as important as taste.

Ambitious bakers are notorious for coming up with bizarre concoctions. Some of these are so successful that they become classics. (No doubt this is how carrot cake got started.) Others go down as well as lead balloons. I once sampled a peach and chili-pepper pie! . . . No comment.

Can you improve on apple pie? Can you reinvent the wheel? This is what keeps enthusiasts coming back year after year, generation after generation. Everyone has a secret ingredient or special trick to make his or her recipe stand out. This section is about just that. These traditional country fair favorites all have something unique about them that made them memorable to me.

Country Fair Favorites

❖

Twice-Baked Apple Pie

Strawberry-Rhubarb Pie With Strawberry Hard Sauce

Pear and Plum Crumb Pie

Buttered Pecan Pie

Country Cream Pie Pastry

Egg and Vinegar Pie Pastry

Blueberry Banana Bread

Country Lemonade Muffins

Honey Graham Date Muffins

Orange Blossom Honey Buns

Praline Apple Cake

Tomato Pan Rolls

Apricot Carrot Cake

Classic Pineapple Pandowdy

Sour Cream Chocolate Spice Cake With Penuche Fudge Frosting

Old-Fashioned Double Fudge Brownies With
Brown Sugar–Chocolate Chip Ice Cream

Chocolate Chunk Peanut Butter Blondies

Honey Pecan Pie Bars

Mocha Almond Monster Cookies

TWICE-BAKED APPLE PIE
MAKES ONE 9-INCH PIE

❖

I'm convinced that if it weren't for apple pies, there would be no country fairs. The two are simply inseparable. Through the years I've been asked to judge many a baking contest . . . and many an apple pie. People come up with all kinds of wonderful concoctions incorporating everything from cheddar cheese to caramel candies. But I'm always in search of the quintessential American apple pie. Is the bottom crust crisp or soggy? Is the filling too runny to slice? These are problems that perennially plague apple pies. I was finally impressed by a pie whose success turned out to be simply a matter of technique: it was twice baked! The filling was thickened with cornstarch and baked in a casserole first, allowing the juices to set. The cornstarch gives a beautiful transparency without a floury taste.

---

8 cups cored, peeled, sliced apples (select firm, crisp varieties)
1/2 cup firmly packed light brown sugar
1/2 cup granulated sugar
3 tablespoons cornstarch
1/2 teaspoon salt
1 teaspoon cinnamon
1/2 teaspoon nutmeg
1/4 cup (1/2 stick) unsalted butter, melted
2 tablespoons lemon juice
COUNTRY CREAM PIE PASTRY (double crust, page 7)
1 egg beaten with 2 tablespoons of water

Preheat oven to 400°F (200°C). Butter 3-quart baking dish. Place apples in large bowl. Combine sugars, cornstarch, salt, and spices in small bowl. Pour over apples and toss to coat. Combine melted butter and lemon juice. Pour over apple mixture and toss. Spoon into prepared dish. Cover apples with sheet of aluminum foil, pressing foil against surface of apples. Cut large vents in foil. Bake 35 minutes. Remove foil and gently stir apples. Cool to room temperature.

Spoon filling into pastry-lined 9-inch deep-dish pie plate, heaping in center. Roll out remaining pastry and drape over filling. Trim edges of pastry to 3/4-inch overhang. Turn under and crimp. Cut vents in top crust. Brush egg-and-water glaze over center of pie (not on crimped edges). Cover edges with strips of aluminum foil. Bake 20 minutes. Remove foil strips and continue baking until crust is golden, 20 to 30 minutes. Cool at least 45 minutes before slicing.

Strawberry-Rhubarb Pie With Strawberry Hard Sauce
makes one 9-inch pie

❖

This quintessential summer pie is always a hit at country fairs. I like the contrast of the tart filling topped with sweet hard sauce. As with apple pies, strawberry-rhubarb pies can have "soggy bottom" problems. That's why I favor this recipe. The filling is first cooked on top of the stove so it won't water down the bottom crust.

3 cups fresh rhubarb, cut into 1/2-inch pieces
2 cups fresh strawberries, halved
1 1/4 cups sugar
3 tablespoons cornstarch
1/4 teaspoon salt
1/4 teaspoon nutmeg
COUNTRY CREAM PIE PASTRY (double crust, page 7)
1 to 2 teaspoons sugar
STRAWBERRY HARD SAUCE (recipe follows)

Combine rhubarb, strawberries, sugar, tapioca, salt, and nutmeg in large saucepan and let stand 15 to 20 minutes. Bring mixture to boil and stir gently until thickened. Remove from heat and cool 1 hour.

Preheat oven to 375°F (190°C). Spoon filling into pastry-lined 9-inch pie plate. Roll out remaining pastry and drape over filling. Trim edges of pastry to 3/4-inch overhang. Turn under and crimp. Cover edges with strips of aluminum foil. Cut vents in the top crust and sprinkle lightly with 1 to 2 teaspoons of sugar. Bake 30 minutes. Remove foil strips and continue baking until pastry is golden brown, 10 to 15 minutes. Cool at least 45 minutes before slicing. Top with scoops of hard sauce.

Strawberry Hard Sauce

1/2 cup (1 stick) unsalted butter
1 1/2 cups powdered sugar
1/4 cup chopped strawberries

Cream butter with electric mixer until light and fluffy. Beat in powdered sugar and strawberries. Chill if serving on warm pie.

Opposite: *Twice-Baked Apple Pie, page 3*

PEAR AND PLUM CRUMB PIE
MAKES ONE 9-INCH PIE

❖

Plums add a rosy blush to fresh pears when they're baked together. Topped with a crunchy pecan streusel, this pie is a winner!

1/2 cup sugar
1/3 cup all-purpose flour
1/2 teaspoon mace
1/4 teaspoon nutmeg
2 cups cored, peeled, sliced pears
2 cups sliced red or purple plums
EGG AND VINEGAR PIE PASTRY (single crust, page 8)
PECAN CRUMB TOPPING (recipe follows)

Preheat oven to 425°F (220°C). Combine sugar, flour, and spices in large mixing bowl. Add pears and plums, tossing gently to coat. Spoon filling into pastry-lined 9-inch pie plate (crimp edges of pastry as high as possible). Cover edges with strips of aluminum foil. Spread pecan crumb topping over filling. Bake 30 minutes. Remove foil strips and continue baking until crust is golden brown, 10 to 20 minutes. Cool at least 45 minutes before slicing.

PECAN CRUMB TOPPING

3/4 cup all-purpose flour
1/3 cup firmly packed light brown sugar
1/3 cup chilled unsalted butter, cut into cubes
1/2 cup chopped, toasted pecans*

Combine flour and brown sugar in mixing bowl. Cut in butter with pastry blender until crumbly. Stir in pecans.

NOTE: Toast pecans in 375°F (190°C) oven for 5 to 10 minutes, stirring 3 times while baking.

Opposite: Buttered Pecan Pie, page 6

BUTTERED PECAN PIE
MAKES ONE 9-INCH PIE

❖

There are pecan pies . . . and there are pecan pies! What makes one better than the other? Technique. The same ingredients that give one pie the taste of a heavenly praline makes another taste like sweet, gooey glue studded with green, chewy pecans. The best pecan pies always feature roasted nuts. Browned butter brings out even more flavor, which is what makes this pie so special.

1/4 cup (1/2 stick) unsalted butter
3/4 cup heavy cream
1 cup firmly packed light brown sugar
1/4 teaspoon salt
1/2 cup light corn syrup
1 teaspoon vanilla
3 eggs
11/2 cups toasted pecan halves*
EGG AND VINEGAR PIE PASTRY (single crust, page 8)

Preheat oven to 375°F (190°C). Heat butter in medium saucepan over low until it turns golden amber; do not burn. Immediately pour cream into butter to stop cooking. Pour into mixing bowl. Blend in brown sugar, salt, corn syrup, and vanilla. Beat in eggs by hand until well blended. Stir in pecans. Pour into pastry-lined 9-inch pie plate (crimp edges of pastry as high as possible). Cover edges with strips of aluminum foil. Bake 30 minutes. Remove foil strips and continue baking until filling is set and pastry is golden, 15 to 20 minutes. Cool at least 2 hours before slicing.

NOTE: Toast pecans in 375°F (190°C) oven for 5 to 10 minutes, stirring 3 times while baking.

COUNTRY CREAM PIE PASTRY
MAKES 1 DOUBLE CRUST OR 2 SINGLE CRUSTS FOR 9-INCH PIE

❖

Typical pie pastry is made with flour, shortening, salt, and water. It requires a light touch or the end result is tough. This rich, country-style recipe replaces that water with half-and-half. The pastry is so tender and flaky that a beginning baker will feel like a pro. To make one single-crust pie shell, simply cut the recipe in half (see below).

$2^2/3$ cups all-purpose flour
$1/2$ to 1 teaspoon salt
1 cup butter-flavored shortening
7 to 8 tablespoons very cold half-and-half

Combine flour and salt in mixing bowl. Cut in until mixture resembles small peas. Add half-and-half a spoonful at a time, tossing lightly with fork; add just enough so that dough clings.

Divide dough in half; gently press each half into a ball. Roll out each ball, one at a time, into 12-inch circle (for best results, I recommend using floured pastry cloth and rolling pin stocking). Ease bottom crust into 9-inch pie plate, allowing surplus pastry to overhang. Add filling and cover with second pastry circle. Trim edges to $3/4$ inch, turn under and crimp.

SINGLE-CRUST PIE

Prepare half of recipe using $1^1/3$ cups flour, $1/2$ cup shortening, $1/4$ to $1/2$ teaspoon salt and 3 to 4 tablespoons half-and-half. Line pie plate with pastry circle, allowing surplus pastry to overhang. Trim edges to $3/4$ inch, turn under and crimp.

EGG AND VINEGAR PIE PASTRY
MAKES 1 DOUBLE CRUST OR 1 SINGLE CRUST FOR 9-INCH PIE

❖

Use this pastry in any pie recipe calling for uncooked fruit filling: the egg helps the bottom crust hold up under juicy fillings. Even though it's not quite as flaky as Country Cream Pie Pastry, this pastry is less fragile. It's also very easy to handle.

3 cups all-purpose flour
1 teaspoon salt
1 1/4 cups butter-flavored shortening
1 egg, beaten
5 tablespoons cold water
1 tablespoon white vinegar

Combine flour and salt in mixing bowl. Cut in until mixture resembles small peas. Combine egg, water, and vinegar in glass measuring cup. Add all at once to flour mixture, tossing with fork until flour is evenly moistened. Gather dough into 3 equal-size balls. Roll out as described in Country Cream Pie Pastry (page 7).

BLUEBERRY BANANA BREAD
MAKES ONE 9 × 5 × 3-INCH OR TWO 8$^1/2$ × 4$^1/2$ × 2-INCH LOAVES

— ❖ —

I usually bake at least two of these loaves at a time. It freezes so well that I like to keep one on hand for an impromptu hostess gift. Blueberry banana bread will always make you a welcome guest!

1/2 cup (1 stick) unsalted butter, softened
3/4 cup granulated sugar
1/2 cup firmly packed light brown sugar
2 eggs
1$^1/2$ cups mashed ripe banana (3 to 4 medium)
1/2 cup buttermilk
1 teaspoon vanilla
2$^1/2$ cups all-purpose flour
1 teaspoon baking soda
1/2 teaspoon salt
1/2 teaspoon nutmeg
1/2 cup chopped toasted walnuts*
1 cup fresh blueberries

Preheat oven to 350°F (180°C). Grease bottoms only of one 9 × 5 × 3-inch or two 8$^1/2$ × 4$^1/2$ × 2-inch loaf pans, or line bottom with baking parchment. (If using disposable foil pans, simply coat bottom with nonstick cooking spray.)

Cream butter with sugars in mixing bowl. Beat in eggs, banana, buttermilk, and vanilla. Combine flour, baking soda, salt, and nutmeg in separate bowl. Add to banana mixture with walnuts and blueberries and stir gently, just until all ingredients are moistened; do not overmix. Bake until toothpick inserted in center comes out clean, about 1$^1/4$ hours for 9-inch or 1 hour for 8$^1/2$-inch loaves. Cool 5 minutes, then remove bread from pan and cool completely. (If using disposable foil pans, cool bread in pan.) Keep tightly wrapped and store in refrigerator for easier slicing.

NOTE: Toast walnuts in 375°F (190°C) oven for 5 to 10 minutes, stirring 3 times while baking.

COUNTRY LEMONADE MUFFINS
MAKES 1 DOZEN MUFFINS

❖

These delightfully tart muffins often pop up at country fair bake sale tables. I've even bought them from some little girls running a roadside lemonade stand. They really are an easy and delicious classic. Serve them any time, for breakfast or dessert.

---

2 cups all-purpose flour
5 tablespoons sugar
1 tablespoon plus 1 teaspoon poppy seed
1 tablespoon baking powder
$^{1}/_{2}$ teaspoon salt
$^{1}/_{2}$ cup frozen lemonade concentrate, thawed
(from 6-ounce can;
reserve remainder for glaze)
$^{1}/_{2}$ cup milk
$^{1}/_{3}$ cup melted butter
1 egg
LEMONADE GLAZE (recipe follows)

Preheat oven to 400°F (200°C). Grease bottoms only of 12 muffin cups, or line with paper liners. Combine flour, sugar, poppy seed, baking powder, and salt in mixing bowl. Combine lemonade concentrate, milk, butter, and egg in glass measuring cup and beat with fork until blended. Pour into flour mixture and stir with fork just until dry ingredients are well moistened; do not overmix. Fill muffin cups $^{3}/_{4}$ full. Bake until golden brown, and a toothpick inserted in the center comes out clean, 15 to 20 minutes.

Immediately remove from pan. Pierce top of each muffin 3 times with fork. Spoon a teaspoon of glaze over top of each muffin; glaze will crystallize on top as it cools.

LEMONADE GLAZE

$^{1}/_{4}$ cup reserved lemonade concentrate
$^{1}/_{4}$ cup sugar

Combine concentrate and sugar in small saucepan and heat until sugar dissolves (or heat in glass measuring cup in microwave). Spoon hot glaze over warm muffins.

HONEY GRAHAM DATE MUFFINS
MAKES ABOUT TEN 2¹/₂-INCH MUFFINS

❖

This is an interesting version of another muffin classic. There's no flour in the recipe, just graham cracker crumbs. Nothing could be quicker to mix.

2¹/₂ cups honey graham cracker crumbs
¹/₄ cup firmly packed dark brown sugar
2 teaspoons baking powder
1 cup whole milk
1 egg
2 tablespoons honey
¹/₂ cup chopped, pitted dates
¹/₂ cup toasted chopped pecans*

Preheat oven to 400°F (200°C). Grease 10 muffin cups, or line with paper liners. In a medium-size mixing bowl, combine graham cracker crumbs, brown sugar, and baking powder. In a glass measuring cup, combine milk, egg, and honey. Beat with a fork to blend egg. Pour liquid ingredients over dry ingredients. Add dates and pecans. Stir just until moistened. Fill muffin cups about ²/₃ full. Bake 15 to 18 minutes, or until a toothpick inserted in the center comes out clean. Let stand 5 minutes before removing muffins from pan.

NOTE: Toast pecans in a 375°F (190°C) oven for 5 to 10 minutes, stirring 3 times while baking.

Orange Blossom Honey Buns
MAKES 9 BUNS

✦

Honey buns, sticky buns, and caramel rolls all have one thing in common—a rich, gooey glaze no one can resist! Just like a pineapple upside-down cake, the best part is on the bottom. When the pan turns over, all that "good stuff" runs down the sides. This version is made with a syrup of fresh orange, brown sugar, honey, and butter, and topped with toasted almonds.

1/3 cup firmly packed light brown sugar
1/3 cup granulated sugar
2 tablespoons honey
3 tablespoons unsalted butter
2 tablespoons orange juice
2 tablespoons finely shredded orange peel
1/2 cup lightly toasted almonds*
2 cups all-purpose flour
1 tablespoon baking powder
1/2 teaspoon salt
1/3 cup butter-flavored shortening
3/4 cup milk
1/4 cup granulated sugar
1/2 teaspoon cinnamon

Coat 8-inch square pan with nonstick cooking spray. Combine 1/3 cup each light brown and granulated sugar with honey, butter, orange juice, and 1 tablespoon of orange peel in small saucepan and bring to boil. Simmer 1 minute, stirring. Remove 2 tablespoons syrup and set aside. Pour remaining syrup into prepared pan. Sprinkle almonds evenly over syrup. Stir together flour, baking powder, salt, and reserved orange peel in mixing bowl. Cut in shortening until mixture resembles coarse crumbs. Make well in center and pour in milk all at once. Stir just until dough clings together in ball. Turn dough out onto lightly floured surface and knead gently 15 to 20 times. Roll out on floured surface into a 9 × 12-inch rectangle. Spread dough with reserved orange syrup. Mix 1/4 cup sugar with cinnamon and sprinkle over syrup. Roll up jelly roll style, beginning with long side. Slice into 9 equal sections. Arrange slices cut side down on syrup in pan.

Preheat oven to 425°F (220°C). Bake until golden, about 20 minutes. Loosen sides with metal spatula, and invert buns onto plate or tray.

*NOTE: Toast almonds in a 375°F (190°C) oven for 5 to 10 minutes, stirring 3 times while baking.

Opposite: Blueberry Banana Bread, page 9

Praline Apple Cake
MAKES ONE 9-INCH LAYER CAKE

❖

*T*his is one of my favorite country layer cakes. You see a lot of apple and spice combinations
at fall festivals, and many of them are quite similar. I think the browned butter glaze
makes this one stand out—it tastes like a caramel apple.

$^1/_2$ cup (1 stick) unsalted butter
1 cup granulated sugar
$^1/_2$ cup firmly packed dark brown sugar
2 eggs
2 cups all-purpose flour
2 teaspoons baking soda
2 teaspoons cinnamon
1 teaspoon nutmeg
$^1/_2$ teaspoon salt
4 cups cored, peeled, finely chopped apple
1$^1/_2$ cups chopped, toasted pecans*
BROWNED BUTTER GLAZE (recipe follows)

Preheat oven to 350°F (180°C). Line bottoms
of two 9-inch round cake pans with baking
parchment. Melt butter in medium saucepan.
Remove from heat. Blend in sugars. Add eggs
and beat until smooth. Combine flour, baking
soda, spices, and salt in mixing bowl. Add butter
mixture and blend well. Stir in apple and 1 cup
pecans. Divide batter between prepared pans. Bake
until top springs back when lightly touched, 40 to
45 minutes. Cool completely. Remove from pans
and peel off baking parchment. Spread some glaze
on top of one layer. Sprinkle with $^1/_4$ cup pecans.
Stack second layer on top and spread with
remaining glaze, allowing some to drizzle down
sides. Top with remaining $^1/_4$ cup pecans.

NOTE: Toast pecans in 375°F (190°C) oven for
5 to 10 minutes, stirring 3 times while baking.

BROWNED BUTTER GLAZE

$^1/_3$ cup unsalted butter
3 cups powdered sugar
2 tablespoons milk
2 teaspoons vanilla

Heat butter in medium saucepan over low heat
until it turns golden amber; do not burn. Remove
from heat and whisk in powdered sugar. Blend in
milk and vanilla to form a smooth, spreadable
glaze.

Opposite: Orange Blossom Honey Buns, page 12

TOMATO PAN ROLLS
MAKES ABOUT 2 DOZEN ROLLS

❖

What a surprise to come across these gems at a summer tomato festival. These fairs feature anything and everything you could possibly do with tomatoes. Bursting with herbs and a cheesy crust, these rolls are perfect on a July evening with a pasta salad, or on a January night with a hearty bowl of soup. Best of all, you don't have to find a ripe tomato to bake them.

2 cups plus 1 tablespoon water
1/4 cup tomato paste
1/2 teaspoon dried basil
1/2 teaspoon dried dill
1/4 teaspoon garlic powder
1 cup rolled oats
3 tablespoons unsalted butter
3 3/4 to 4 3/4 cups all-purpose flour
1/4 cup sugar
2 teaspoons salt
2 envelopes active dry yeast
1 egg
6 tablespoons unsalted butter, melted
HERB-CHEESE TOPPING (recipe follows)

Grease a 9 × 13-inch baking pan. Bring water to boil in medium saucepan. Blend in tomato paste, herbs, and garlic powder. Stir in oats. Remove from heat and stir in butter. Let mixture cool to about 130°F to 120°F (55°C to 50°C).

Combine 1 1/2 cups flour, sugar, salt, and yeast in a large bowl. Add tomato mixture and egg. Blend with mixer at low speed until moistened, then beat 3 minutes at medium speed. Stir in 1 3/4 cups to 2 1/2 cups flour, using enough to form stiff dough. On floured surface (or in electric mixer fitted with dough hook), knead in remaining 1/2 to 3/4 cup flour until dough is smooth and elastic (about 5 minutes). Shape dough into ball. Cover with large bowl and let rest 15 minutes. Punch down to remove all air bubbles. Pat dough evenly into prepared pan. Using sharp knife, score dough into 2-inch squares. Cover loosely with greased plastic wrap and cloth towel. Let rise in warm place until doubled in bulk.

Preheat oven to 375°F (190°C). Uncover pan and recut dough by poking tip of sharp knife into scored lines (do not pull knife through dough or it will deflate). Brush 4 tablespoons butter over rolls and bake 15 minutes. Brush with remaining 2 tablespoons butter, sprinkle with herb-cheese topping, and bake until topping is golden, 10 to 15 minutes; do not let spices burn. Serve warm or at room temperature.

HERB-CHEESE TOPPING

1 tablespoon grated Parmesan cheese
$1/2$ teaspoon dried basil
$1/2$ teaspoon dried dill
$1/4$ teaspoon garlic powder

Combine all ingredients in small dish.

Apricot Carrot Cake
MAKES ONE 13 × 9-INCH CAKE

❖

Carrot cake has become classic country fair fare. It's probably even more American than apple pie. In a sea of carrot cakes, what makes this one memorable? For starters, sautéed walnuts and wholewheat flour give it a truly nutty taste and texture. Instead of raisins, it's studded with tangy morsels of apricot. But the frosting is the best part: it's sweetened with apricot jam instead of the usual powdered sugar.

1 cup chopped walnuts
1/4 cup (1 stick) unsalted butter
1 cup granulated sugar
1 cup firmly packed light brown sugar
3/4 cup vegetable oil
1 teaspoon vanilla
4 eggs
1 1/2 cups wholewheat pastry flour
1/2 cup all-purpose flour
1 teaspoon baking soda
1 teaspoon baking powder
1 teaspoon salt
1 teaspoon cinnamon
1 teaspoon nutmeg
3 cups finely shredded carrot
3/4 cup finely chopped dried apricots
APRICOT CHEESE FROSTING (recipe follows)

Preheat oven to 350°F (180°C). Grease and flour 13 × 9-inch baking pan. Sauté walnuts in butter in skillet, until golden; do not burn. Set aside to cool slightly. Combine sugars, oil, vanilla, and eggs in large bowl and beat at medium speed until well blended, about 1 1/2 minutes. Stir in walnuts and butter. Combine flours, baking soda, baking powder, salt, and spices in separate bowl. Stir into egg mixture with carrot and apricots. Pour into prepared pan. Bake until toothpick inserted in center comes out clean, 45 to 50 minutes. Remove cake from oven and reduce temperature to 300°F (150°C). Cool cake 10 minutes, then spread evenly with frosting. Bake another 5 more minutes. Cool completely before slicing.

Apricot Cheese Frosting

one 8-oz and one 3-oz package cream cheese, softened
1/2 teaspoon vanilla
1/4 teaspoon almond extract
6 tablespoons apricot jam

Beat cream cheese with extracts until soft and fluffy. Beat in jam 1 tablespoon at a time.

CLASSIC PINEAPPLE PANDOWDY
MAKES ONE 10-INCH CAKE

❖

This old-fashioned dessert is still a country fair favorite. The familiar pineapple upside-down cake started around the turn of the century; back then, it was baked in a skillet with an ovenproof handle. The hot pandowdy was turned upside down, revealing a gooey caramelized topping. I like the way the brown sugar batter in this recipe complements the pralined pineapple.

1/4 cup (1/2 stick) unsalted butter
2/3 cup firmly packed light brown sugar
16-ounce can sliced pineapple, well drained
9 pecan halves
1 1/3 cups all-purpose flour
1 cup firmly packed light brown sugar
1 1/2 teaspoon baking powder
1/2 teaspoon salt
1/3 cup butter-flavored shortening
1 teaspoon vanilla
3/4 cup milk
1 egg

Preheat oven to 350°F (180°C). Melt butter in 10-inch skillet with ovenproof handle (or use 9-inch square baking pan). Sprinkle 2/3 cup brown sugar over butter. Arrange 9 pineapple slices in skillet: 1 ring in the center, surrounded by 8. (If using square pan, arrange pineapple in 3 rows of 3.) Place pecan half in center of each pineapple ring. Combine flour, 1 cup brown sugar, baking powder and salt in large mixing bowl. Add shortening, vanilla, milk, and egg and beat at low speed of electric mixer, for 30 seconds. Scrape sides of bowl with rubber spatula, then beat at high speed 2 minutes. Scrape bowl with rubber spatula, and beat at high speed 1 more minute. Pour batter over pineapple. Bake until toothpick inserted in center comes out clean, 45 to 50 minutes (50 to 55 minutes for square pan). Immediately invert on platter. Serve warm or at room temperature.

Sour Cream Chocolate Spice Cake With Penuche Fudge Frosting

Makes One 8-Inch Layer Cake

❖

Chocolate and cinnamon seem to belong together; one brings out the best in the other. Or maybe the best part of this cake is the brown sugar–penuche fudge frosting? I can't decide. I only know that this is my all-time favorite country fair chocolate cake.

1³/4 cups all-purpose flour
³/4 cup granulated sugar
1 cup firmly packed dark brown sugar
³/4 cup Dutch-process cocoa
1¹/2 teaspoons baking soda
1 teaspoon salt
2 teaspoons cinnamon
²/3 cup unsalted butter, softened
1¹/2 cups sour cream
2 eggs
1 teaspoon vanilla
Penuche Fudge Frosting (recipe follows)

Preheat oven to 350°F (180°C). Line two 8-inch round pans with baking parchment. Combine flour, sugars, cocoa, baking soda, salt, and cinnamon in large mixing bowl. Add butter, sour cream, eggs, and vanilla and beat at low speed of electric mixer for 30 seconds. Scrape sides of bowl with rubber spatula and beat at high speed 2 minutes. Scrape bowl with rubber spatula and beat 1 minute longer. Pour batter into prepared pans and bake until toothpick inserted in center comes out clean, 35 to 40 minutes. Cool layers completely. Remove from pans and peel off baking parchment. Fill and frost sides and top with frosting.

Penuche Fudge Frosting

¹/2 cup (1 stick) unsalted butter
1 cup firmly packed dark brown sugar
¹/4 cup milk
2 cups powdered sugar

Melt butter in large saucepan. Blend in brown sugar and bring to boil, stirring constantly. Simmer over low heat for 2 minutes, stirring. Stir in milk and return to boil. Remove from heat and cool until mixture is lukewarm to touch. Slowly whisk in powdered sugar. Place pan in bowl of ice water and beat until frosting is of spreading consistency. If frosting becomes too stiff to spread, beat in a few drops of milk.

Old-Fashioned Double Fudge Brownies With Brown Sugar–Chocolate Chip Ice Cream

MAKES 16 BROWNIES

❖

These brownies are worthy of a blue ribbon. They're my ultimate childhood chocolate fantasy come true. The dense, fudgy batter is rich with brown sugar. The glaze on top tastes like a hot fudge sundae. I had the good fortune of trying these at a fair where they were being served with brown sugar–chocolate chip ice cream. This caramel ice cream, studded with chocolate, reminded me of cookie dough. The combination was incredible!

---

4 ounces unsweetened chocolate
3/4 cup (1 1/2 sticks) unsalted butter
1 cup granulated sugar
1 cup firmly packed dark brown sugar
3 eggs
1 teaspoon vanilla
1 cup all purpose flour
CHOCOLATE GLAZE (recipe follows)
BROWN SUGAR–CHOCOLATE CHIP ICE
CREAM (recipe follows)

Preheat oven to 350°F (180°C). Lightly grease 9-inch square pan or line bottom with baking parchment. Combine chocolate and butter in large saucepan, and melt over very low heat, stirring until smooth. Blend in sugars. Remove from heat and beat in eggs and vanilla. Blend in flour. Spread batter in prepared pan. Bake until toothpick inserted in center comes out with fudgy crumbs, about 50 minutes; do not overbake. Cool brownies for about 20 minutes, then spread with warm glaze. Cool completely before cutting. Serve with ice cream.

Chocolate Glaze

1/3 cup unsalted butter
2 ounces unsweetened chocolate
2 cups powdered sugar
2 teaspoons vanilla
2 to 4 tablespoons hot water

Combine butter and chocolate in medium saucepan and melt over low heat. Remove from heat; blend in powdered sugar and vanilla. Stir in water 1 tablespoon at a time until mixture reaches glaze consistency.

BROWN SUGAR–CHOCOLATE CHIP ICE CREAM
MAKES 1 QUART

❖

3/4 cup firmly packed dark brown sugar
1/4 teaspoon salt
1 cup milk
3 egg yolks, beaten
1 tablespoon vanilla
2 cups very cold heavy cream
1 cup coarsely chopped chocolate
chips (milk or semisweet)

Combine brown sugar, salt, milk, and egg yolks in large saucepan, and cook over medium heat, whisking frequently, just until bubbles appear around edge. Cool to room temperature. Stir in vanilla and cream. Chill several hours. Transfer mixture to ice cream maker and process according to manufacturer's directions. As ice cream begins to harden, add chocolate chips and continue to churn. Serve immediately or pack ice cream into a 1-quart container and freeze.

*Opposite: Apricot Carrot Cake With Apricot
Cheese Frosting, page 16*

CHOCOLATE CHUNK PEANUT BUTTER BLONDIES
MAKES 3 DOZEN BLONDIES

———— ❖ ————

*T*hese are simply heaven for peanut butter lovers. Although you can use semi-sweet chocolate chips in the recipe, I love the flavor and texture of coarsely chopped dark sweet chocolate bars.

one 6-ounce bar (or 1 1/2 4-ounce bars)
of dark sweet chocolate
2/3 cup unsalted butter, softened
2/3 cup creamy peanut butter
1 cup sugar
1 1/2 cups firmly packed light brown sugar
1 teaspoon vanilla
3 eggs
2 1/4 cups all-purpose flour
2 1/2 teaspoons baking powder
1/2 teaspoon salt
PEANUT BUTTER CHOCOLATE GLAZE
(recipe follows)

Preheat oven to 350°F (180°C). Lightly grease the bottom of a 10 × 15-inch baking pan or line bottom with baking parchment. Coarsely chop chocolate bar and set aside while preparing batter. Combine butter and peanut butter in a large mixing bowl. Add sugar, brown sugar, and vanilla. Cream together until light and fluffy. Beat in eggs, one at a time. In a separate bowl, combine flour with baking powder and salt.

Blend flour mixture into peanut butter mixture. Stir in chopped chocolate. Spread batter into prepared pan. Bake 35 minutes and remove from oven. Spread with warm glaze. Cool completely before cutting.

PEANUT BUTTER CHOCOLATE GLAZE

one 6-ounce bar (or 1 1/2 4-ounce bars)
of dark sweet chocolate
1/3 cup creamy peanut butter

Coarsely chop chocolate bar. Combine chocolate and peanut butter in a small saucepan. Cook over very low heat, stirring constantly, until chocolate is melted and mixture is smooth and creamy.

Opposite: Sour Cream Chocolate Spice Cake With Penuche Fudge Frosting, page 18

Honey Pecan Pie Bars
MAKES 3 DOZEN BARS

❖

*T*his popular bar is a hybrid; half cookie, half candy, and 100 percent addictive. The chewy-gooey filling will remind you of a cross between pecan pie and pralines without the hassle of a candy thermometer.

¹/₃ cup powdered sugar
¹/₃ cup firmly packed light brown sugar
2 cups all-purpose flour
1 cup (2 sticks) unsalted butter, softened
HONEY PECAN TOPPING (recipe follows)

Preheat oven to 350°F (190°C). Line a 9 × 13-inch baking pan with parchment. (It's too difficult to remove these bars if you simply grease the pan.) Combine powdered sugar and brown sugar in a large mixing bowl. Blend in flour. Cut butter into dry mixture, until it resembles coarse meal. Pat crust into prepared pan. Bake for 20 minutes. Remove from oven and spread topping evenly over crust and bake 25 minutes longer. Cool completely before cutting into squares.

HONEY PECAN TOPPING

²/₃ cup unsalted butter
¹/₂ cup honey
3 tablespoons heavy cream
1 teaspoon vanilla
¹/₂ cup firmly packed light brown sugar
3¹/₂ cups coarsely chopped, lightly toasted pecans*

Combine butter and honey in a large saucepan and melt together over a low heat. Remove from heat. Stir in cream, vanilla, brown sugar, and pecans.

NOTE: Toast pecans in a 375°F (190°C) oven for 5 to 8 minutes, stirring three times while baking. For this recipe, you want the pecans to be barely tinged with gold. They'll continue to brown while the filling bakes.

Mocha Almond Monster Cookies
Makes about 22 cookies

❖

*B*ig chocolate chip cookies are a big deal these days. Long before there were cookie shops at the mall, there were country fairs where ambitious bakers tried to put a new spin on an American classic. I like this version because the chocolate, coffee, and roasted almond combination reminds me of my favorite ice cream: mocha almond fudge. These are large cookies, so don't try to crowd too many on the baking sheet. Be patient and make several batches . . . They're worth the wait!

two 6-ounce bars (or three 4-ounce bars)
of dark sweet chocolate
1 cup (2 sticks) unsalted butter, softened
1/2 cup sugar
1 cup firmly packed light brown sugar
2 teaspoons instant coffee powder*
2 eggs
1 teaspoon vanilla
2 1/4 cups flour
1 teaspoon baking soda
1 teaspoon salt
1 1/2 cups coarsely chopped, lightly
toasted, *unblanched* almonds**

For best results, cut 4 sheets of baking parchment the size of your baking sheet. You can drop one batch of cookies onto the paper while another is baking. You can also slide the cookies (while they are on the parchment) on a rack to cool. This allows you to re-use your baking sheet. Removing large cookies from paper is far easier than prying them loose from a baking sheet.

Preheat oven to 375°F (190°C). Coarsely chop chocolate bars and set aside. Combine butter, sugar, brown sugar, and instant coffee powder in large mixing bowl. Cream until light and fluffy. Beat in eggs, one at a time. Combine flour, baking soda, and salt in a separate mixing bowl. Blend flour mixture into egg mixture. Stir in chopped chocolate and almonds.

Drop by 1/4 cupfuls (or use an ice cream scoop) onto parchment sheet. Do not crowd or try to bake more than 5 or 6 cookies on one sheet. Lightly press down into 3-inch circles. Bake 10 to 12 minutes, or until edges are lightly browned. Cool cookies on parchment paper before removing.

HELPFUL HINT: Do not use freeze-dried coffee granules! If you must, dissolve granules in a teaspoon of boiling water.

NOTE: Toast pecans in 375°F (190°C) oven for 5 to 8 minutes, stirring three times while baking.

PICKLES, PRESERVES, AND PUT-UPS

❖

"Putting up" produce from a bountiful harvest is steeped into our American heritage. It was one of the practical ways to preserve an abundance of food for the lean months of winter. The ritual evolved into an art form. A farm wife could discover fame from prizewinning pickles, and the state fair became a showcase for such talent. Creative combinations of vegetables, fruits, and spices were simmered and sealed into jars. This method, known as water bath processing, is an essential part of all pickling and preserving. Without a proper vacuum seal, food will spoil at room temperature.

The texture and appearance of preserves are almost as important as the taste. In some parts of the country preserves are judged on these qualities alone. It's very important to skim the foam from jelly before filling jars. Conserves and chutneys tend to be a little less temperamental. They don't contain added pectin, but they must be reduced to the proper consistency. "Putting up" is habit forming. Once you get started, there's simply no end to the possibilities. It will also make you very popular with your friends! Just about anything in a jar with a cloth cover tied on top makes a welcome gift.

Water Bath Processing

❖

Equipment

Two-piece lids, one-pint mason jars or half-pint jelly jars, large kettle for sterilizing jars and another kettle or large saucepan for preparing the recipe, tongs, clean dry dish towels, labels, homespun or calico cotton cloth, ribbon or cord.

❖

Sterilizing Jars

This is usually done as the recipe is being prepared on the stove. It's important that the jars be dry but still warm when standing by to be filled. Place jars and loose lids in a large kettle. Fill with water to cover completely. Bring to a rolling boil and boil 10 minutes. Carefully remove jars with tongs and allow water to drain back into kettle. Turn jars upside down on a clean dish towel. Remove lids and jar bands from kettle and drain on dish towel.

❖

Forming a Heat Seal

*Fill warm jars to within $1/4$-inch of the rim. Place lids on jars and screw on bands. Use tongs to place jars **upright** in the kettle of boiling water. Boil for the number of minutes specified in the recipe (usually 5 to 10). Carefully remove jars with tongs, keeping upright at all times. Cool. NOTE: Many jelly and jam recipes simply require inverting the jar, then turning upright to form a seal.*

❖

Finishing Touches

As soon as jars are cool, label them with contents and date they were "put up." Lids may be covered with circles or squares of country cotton tied in place with ribbon or cord.

Pickles, Preserves, and Put-ups

❖

Iced Bread-and-Butter Pickles

Dilly Wax Beans

Country-style Chunky Chili Sauce

Bell Pepper Jelly

Three-Berry Preserves

Spiced Grape Jam

Orange-Rhubarb Jam

Green Apple Chutney

Cranberry-Pear Conserve

Apple-Pumpkin Butter

ICED BREAD-AND-BUTTER PICKLES
MAKES 5 PINTS

❖

A picnic without pickles would be like Thanksgiving without cranberries. No wonder pickle cooking contests became such an important part of summer country fairs. Bread-and-butter pickles are the condiment of choice on barbecue-grilled burgers and usually find their way into the potato salad. Ice keeps the vegetables crisp, while the salt partially brines them.

4 quarts thinly sliced cucumbers
8 onions, sliced
2 green bell peppers, split in half, seeded and sliced
1/2 cup kosher salt
2 trays of ice cubes
4 cups sugar
1 1/2 teaspoons turmeric
1/2 teaspoon ground cloves
4 teaspoons whole mustard seed
1 teaspoon celery seed
4 1/2 cups distilled white vinegar

Combine sugar, spices, and vinegar in large kettle and bring to boil. Reduce heat to very low and add vegetables. Heat through but *do not* allow liquid to boil. Meanwhile, sterilize five 1-pint jars (and loose lids) in another kettle filled with boiling water. Turn jars and lids upside down on clean dish towel to drain. Ladle pickles into hot jars; liquid should come within 1/4-inch of top. Seal lids and process jars in kettle of boiling water for 5 minutes. Remove jars with tongs and cool. Once opened, pickles must be stored in the refrigerator.

Combine cucumbers, onions, and peppers in large bowl. Sprinkle salt over vegetables and toss to coat. Empty trays of ice over vegetables. Let stand 3 hours. Drain vegetables completely.

DILLY WAX BEANS
MAKES 4 PINTS

❖

Pickled beans in dill are a summer delight to savor all year long. The problem with pickling green beans is that they lose their fresh color and turn to olive drab. For this reason, I've always preferred to pickle wax beans. They're already yellow to begin with!

2 pounds wax beans, washed
and trimmed to same length
4 cloves garlic, halved
2 teaspoons whole mustard seed
1 teaspoon cracked pepper
4 heads fresh dill
2$^{1}/_{2}$ cups water
2$^{1}/_{2}$ cups distilled white vinegar
$^{1}/_{4}$ cup kosher salt

pepper to each jar. Tuck a head of dill into each jar, next to beans. Combine water, vinegar, and kosher salt in large saucepan or kettle and bring to rolling boil. Pour hot liquid into jars, filling to $^{1}/_{4}$-inch from top. Seal lids and process jars in kettle of boiling water for 10 minutes. Remove jars with tongs and cool. Once opened, beans must be stored in the refrigerator.

Sterilize four 1-pint glass jars (and loose lids) in kettle filled with boiling water. Turn jars and lids upside down on clean dish towel to drain. Pack beans into hot jars, allowing $^{1}/_{4}$-inch head space. Add 2 half garlic cloves to each jar. Add $^{1}/_{2}$ teaspoon mustard seed and $^{1}/_{4}$ teaspoon

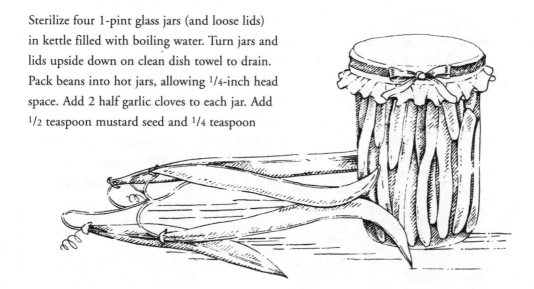

COUNTRY-STYLE CHUNKY CHILI SAUCE
MAKES 6 TO 8 PINTS

❖

Every gardener knows that when tomato season arrives, the tomatoes just keep coming and coming. Soon you're up to your eyeballs in tomatoes! I once brought some over to a friend's house, who was about to bring some over to my house. We both felt silly and a little sad that we'd already become sick of eating such a summer treat. Who wouldn't relish just one vine-ripened tomato in January? But we were in the midst of a tomato population explosion. The solution: turn them into chili sauce. Try it on a hamburger instead of ketchup, and you'll appreciate your tomato crop all year long.

4 quarts tomatoes, peeled and chopped
1 cup chopped red bell pepper
1 cup chopped green bell pepper
1 cup chopped yellow bell pepper
2 cups chopped onion
1/2 cup minced celery
1 tablespoon celery seed
1 tablespoon mustard seed
1 bay leaf
1 teaspoon whole cloves
1 teaspoon ground ginger
1 teaspoon nutmeg
2 cinnamon sticks
3 cups cider vinegar
1 1/2 cups sugar
2 tablespoons salt

Combine tomatoes, peppers, onion, celery, celery seed, and mustard seed in large kettle. Tie bay leaf, cloves, ginger, nutmeg, and cinnamon sticks in cheesecloth bag. Add bag to kettle along with vinegar, sugar, and salt. Bring mixture to boil. Reduce heat and simmer until sauce is very thick, 1 1/2 to 2 hours, stirring frequently. Meanwhile, sterilize six to eight 1-pint glass jars (and loose lids) in another kettle filled with boiling water. Turn jars and lids upside down on clean dish towel to drain. Ladle sauce into hot jars, leaving 1/4-inch head space. Seal lids and process jars in kettle of boiling water for 15 minutes. Remove jars with tongs and cool. Once opened, sauce must be stored in the refrigerator.

BELL PEPPER JELLY
MAKES 8 HALF-PINTS

❖

*P*epper jelly is more popular now than ever before. Although it has been around for ages, it's as if the world has suddenly discovered it. Served with cream cheese and crackers, it's a staple at parties. It spices up all types of dips and salad dressings. Baste it on grilled chicken or pork for a zesty glaze.

$^1/_2$ cup minced red bell pepper
$^1/_2$ cup minced yellow bell pepper
$6^1/_2$ cups sugar
$1^1/_2$ cups distilled white vinegar
2 pouches (3 ounces each) liquid pectin

Sterilize eight half-pint jars (and loose lids) in kettle filled with boiling water. Turn jars upside down on clean dish towel to drain. Meanwhile, combine peppers, sugar and vinegar in another large kettle and bring to rolling boil. Remove from heat and let stand 5 minutes. Using metal spoon, skim off any foam. Return kettle to heat and bring to second rolling boil. Add pectin, stirring constantly, and boil exactly 1 minute. Ladle jelly into hot jars, leaving $^1/_8$-inch head space. Seal with hot lids and invert jars for 1 minute, then stand upright to cool. Once opened, jelly must be stored in the refrigerator.

Three-Berry Preserves
Makes 6 half-pints

--- ❖ ---

I love the combination of strawberries, raspberries, and blueberries all boiled together in a glorious burst of flavor. Chambord liqueur adds an elegant touch that elevates this above ordinary jam. I even use these preserves as a topping for cheesecake.

> 1 quart fresh strawberries
> 1 quart fresh red raspberries
> 1 quart fresh blueberries
> 1 cup Chambord or other raspberry liqueur
> 2 tablespoons lemon juice
> 1 box (1³⁄4 ounces) powdered pectin
> 6 cups sugar

Sterilize six half-pint jars (and loose lids) in kettle filled with boiling water. Turn jars and lids upside down on clean dish towel to drain. Meanwhile, wash berries; split strawberries in half. Combine berries, Chambord, lemon juice, and pectin in large saucepan and bring to rolling boil, stirring constantly. Stir in sugar and bring back to a boil that can't be stirred down. Boil exactly 1 minute. Immediately remove from heat and skim off any foam with a metal spoon. Ladle into hot jars, leaving ¹⁄8-inch head space. Seal with hot lids and invert jars for 1 minute, then stand upright to cool. Once opened, preserves must be stored in the refrigerator.

SPICED GRAPE JAM
MAKES 4 HALF-PINTS

❖

I confess . . . I'm one of those adults who regarded grape jam as "kid stuff." Once I outgrew peanut butter sandwiches, it didn't seem to serve any purpose. Thanks to a country fair and this recipe, I rediscovered what I'd been missing all these years.

1$\frac{1}{2}$ pounds Concord or Ribier grapes
$\frac{2}{3}$ cup apple juice
4 cups sugar
$\frac{1}{4}$ teaspoon cinnamon
$\frac{1}{8}$ teaspoon nutmeg
$\frac{1}{8}$ teaspoon allspice
1 pouch (3 ounces) liquid pectin
2 tablespoons lime juice

Stem and wash grapes. Drain in colander until dry. Split grapes in half and discard seeds. Coarsely chop grapes in food processor. Combine grapes and apple juice in large saucepan and bring to boil. Simmer, stirring occasionally, until skins are fairly soft and mixture measures about 2 cups, 20 to 30 minutes. Using metal spoon, skim off any foam. Meanwhile, sterilize four half-pint glass jars (and loose lids) in kettle filled with boiling water. Turn jars and lids upside down on clean dish towel to drain. Add sugar and spices to grape mixture. Combine pectin and lime juice in separate glass measure. Bring grape mixture to rolling boil. Pour in pectin and boil exactly 1 minute, stirring constantly. Remove from heat. Using metal spoon, skim off any foam. Ladle jam into hot jars, leaving $\frac{1}{4}$-inch head space. Seal lids and process jars in kettle of boiling water for 5 minutes. Remove jars with tongs and cool. Once opened, jam must be stored in the refrigerator.

Orange-Rhubarb Jam
MAKES 4 PINTS

❖

Everyone loves strawberry-rhubarb jam, and it's a predictable country fair staple. One day I stopped at a country fair on a specific search for a jar of strawberry-rhubarb jam. Instead I came home with a jar of orange-rhubarb jam. What was I thinking? I wondered the next morning at breakfast. All of my doubts disappeared when I spread it on a toasted English muffin. Orange and rhubarb make a wonderful combination that should be a classic in its own right!

4 pounds rhubarb
8 cups sugar
2 tablespoons grated orange peel
1 1/2 cups fresh orange juice

Wash rhubarb and cut into 1-inch pieces. Toss with sugar in large bowl and let stand 8 to 12 hours or overnight. Transfer to large kettle, stir in orange peel and juice, and heat to boiling. Reduce heat to simmer and cook, stirring frequently, until mixture has thickened, about 30 to 40 minutes. Meanwhile, sterilize four 1-pint glass jars (and loose lids) in another kettle filled with boiling water. Turn jars and lids upside down on clean dish towel to drain. Remove jam from heat. Using metal spoon, skim off any foam. Ladle jam into hot jars, leaving 1/4-inch head space. Seal lids and process jars in kettle of boiling water for 5 minutes. Remove jars with tongs and cool. Once opened, jam must be stored in the refrigerator.

Green Apple Chutney
makes 3 pints

❖

It used to be that people didn't know what to do with chutney. Twice a year they'd pull it out of the cupboard when they cooked curried chicken. Now you see it served as a condiment with all kinds of barbecued and grilled meats. It's wonderful with warm Brie. When mixed with mayonnaise it makes a zesty dip. No wonder chutney is more popular at country fairs than ever before.

6 cups cored, peeled, and diced green apples
1 1/2 cups golden raisins
2 medium-size red bell peppers,
seeded and diced
2 medium-size green bell peppers,
seeded and diced
1 clove garlic, crushed
3 ounces crystallized ginger, chopped
1 1/2 teaspoons salt
1/2 cup lemon juice
3 cups firmly packed light brown sugar
2 tablespoons yellow mustard seed

Combine all ingredients in large kettle and bring to boil. Reduce heat and simmer, stirring frequently, until apples and peppers are tender and mixture is reduced to about 1 1/2 quarts, about 45 minutes to 1 hour. Using metal spoon, skim off any foam. Meanwhile, sterilize three 1-pint glass jars (and loose lids) in another kettle filled with boiling water. Turn jars and lids upside down on clean dish towel to drain. Ladle chutney into hot jars, leaving 1/4-inch head space. Seal lids and process jars in kettle of boiling water for 5 minutes. Remove jars with tongs and cool. Once opened, chutney must be stored in the refrigerator.

CRANBERRY-PEAR CONSERVE
MAKES 4 PINTS

❖

*T*angy cranberries teamed with pears, raisins, and walnuts make any meal a holiday. This traditional Thanksgiving conserve complements poultry and pork in every season.

3 cups (12 ounces) fresh or frozen cranberries
3 cups cubed ripe but firm fresh pears
1/2 cup orange juice
1/2 cup port
1 cup sugar
1 cup firmly packed light brown sugar
1 cup golden raisins
1 cinnamon stick
1 cup toasted walnut halves, slightly broken*

Combine cranberries, pears, orange juice, port, sugars, raisins, and cinnamon stick in large saucepan and bring to boil. Reduce heat and simmer until pears are tender and conserve is slightly thickened, 20 to 25 minutes. Using metal spoon, skim off any foam. Remove cinnamon stick and stir in walnuts. Meanwhile, sterilize four 1-pint glass jars (and loose lids) in kettle filled with boiling water. Turn jars and lids upside down on clean dish towel to drain. Ladle conserve into hot jars, leaving 1/4-inch head space. Seal lids and process jars in kettle of boiling water for 10 minutes. Remove jars with tongs and cool. Once opened, conserve must be stored in the refrigerator.

NOTE: Toast walnuts in a 375°F (190°C) oven for 5 to 10 minutes, stirring 3 times while baking.

Opposite: Old-Fashioned Double Fudge Brownies With Brown Sugar-Chocolate Chip Ice Cream, page 19

APPLE-PUMPKIN BUTTER
MAKES 3 TO 4 PINTS

❖

*A*pple-pumpkin butter is much more than a spread for your morning toast. Try it on pound cake, in tartlet shells, or served warm over vanilla ice cream for a real autumn treat. The recipe yield varies depending on the moisture content of the pumpkin. You may get only 3 pints, but sterilize 4 jars just in case.

6 cups baked pumpkin (or use three,
16-ounce cans solid-pack pumpkin)*
2 cups apple juice
1 1/4 cups firmly packed light brown sugar
1 teaspoon cinnamon
1/2 teaspoon nutmeg
1/2 teaspoon ginger
1/8 teaspoon ground cloves

NOTE: To bake pumpkin, split one large or two medium-size fresh pumpkins into quarters. Discard pulp and seeds. Arrange pieces in roasting pan, cover with foil and bake at 375°F (190°C) until flesh is very tender and much of the moisture has evaporated, 1 1/4 to 1 1/2 hours. Peel pumpkin and purée in processor until very smooth. Measure 6 cups purée; reserve any remainder for another use.

Combine all ingredients in large saucepan and bring to simmer over low heat. Simmer, stirring frequently, until mixture is thick and pudding-like, about 1 1/2 hours. Meanwhile, sterilize four 1-pint glass jars (and loose lids) in another kettle filled with boiling water. Turn jars and lids upside down on clean dish towel to drain. Spoon apple-pumpkin butter into hot jars, leaving 1/4-inch head space. Seal lids and process jars in kettle of boiling water for 10 minutes. Remove jars with tongs and cool. Once opened, butter must be stored in the refrigerator.

Opposite: Dilly Wax Beans, *page 29*

HOLIDAY BAKING BAZAAR

❖

We tend to think of the holidays as that hectic, happy period between Thanksgiving and Christmas. Cookie exchanges and fruitcakes become big business for church and community bazaars. But these organizations will be the first to acknowledge that there are several holiday seasons. In the doldrums of February, there are chocolate festivals to tempt you out of your snowbound house. Saint Patrick's Day is everyone's excuse to bake Irish scones. With Easter comes bunny bread.

Summertime is a hiatus for holiday bazaars, as bakers focus on big-league state and country fairs for displaying their goodies. The Fourth of July is a celebration of pies and tarts. In recent times Halloween has become the great American "pumpkin holiday." At Octoberfests, Pumpkinfests, and "Haunted Open Houses" you'll find fifty ways to cook a pumpkin, along with spooky treats to tempt a sweet tooth.

All around the calendar, every season is worth celebrating, and nothing does it better than a good old-fashioned holiday bazaar. Successful ones are organized to take advantage of all the available talent. Find out who does what best and assign tasks accordingly. People are always proud to contribute their specialty.

Holiday Baking Bazaar

❖

Chocolate Cherry Sweethearts

White Chocolate Amaretto Truffles

President's Day Cherry Pie Squares

St. Patrick's Day Shamrock Scones

Easter Bunny Bread

Hot-Crossed Buns

Star-Spangled Berry Tarts

Fourth of July Lemon Meringue Pie

Colonial Tombstone Cookies

Cranberry Pumpkin Bread

Shaker Sugar-Pumpkin Pie

Cornmeal Pastry Crust and Pastry Pumpkin

Snowmen Meringues

Chocolate Peppermint Pinwheels

Gingerbread Teddy Bears

Candy Cane Coffee Cakes

Christmas Cheesecake

Pistachio-Almond Cake

Fruitcake Hater's Conversion Cake

CHOCOLATE CHERRY SWEETHEARTS
MAKES 3 TO 4 DOZEN

❖

Just when the winter blahs and blizzards have got you down, Valentine's Day comes along. Almost anyone can be cheered up by chocolate, which must be the rationale behind this holiday. As soon as the calorie concerns of Christmas have been reconciled, chocolate festivals crop up everywhere. February is also, by tradition, the cherry month. For this reason I think these cookies are classics.

---

1 cup (2 sticks) unsalted butter, softened
1 cup sugar
$^1/_4$ cup milk
1 egg
1 teaspoon almond extract
$2^3/_4$ cups all-purpose flour
$^1/_2$ cup Dutch-process cocoa
$^3/_4$ teaspoon baking powder
$^1/_4$ teaspoon baking soda
12-ounce jar cherry preserves
ALMOND ICING (recipe follows)

Cream butter and sugar in mixing bowl until light and fluffy. Blend in milk, egg, and almond extract. Combine flour, cocoa, baking powder, and baking soda in separate bowl and stir into butter mixture. Divide dough in thirds. Wrap each in plastic and chill at least 2 hours.

Preheat oven to 350°F (180°C). Line baking sheets with parchment. For best results, use a lightly floured pastry cloth with rolling pin cover. Work with $^1/_3$ of dough at a time, keeping the rest refrigerated. Roll dough out to about

$^1/_8$-inch thick and cut with $2^1/_2$- to 3-inch heart-shaped cookie cutter. Arrange hearts on prepared baking sheets. (Chill scraps of dough and reroll.) Bake until cookies are set, 9 to 11 minutes. Cool on parchment and gently lift off with spatula.

Sandwich cooled cookies, bottoms together, with a teaspoon of cherry preserves. Fill pastry bag, fitted with small writing tip, with almond icing. Drizzle icing back and forth diagonally across cookies, or outline edges of cookies with icing and write *I Love You* or *Be Mine* in the center.

ALMOND ICING

---

2 cups powdered sugar
2 to 3 tablespoons milk
$^1/_2$ teaspoon almond extract
red food coloring

Place powdered sugar in small mixing bowl and blend in enough milk to make smooth icing. Flavor with almond extract and tint pale pink with a tiny amount of red food coloring.

WHITE CHOCOLATE AMARETTO TRUFFLES
MAKES 3 TO 4 DOZEN

❖

*It just wouldn't be Valentine's Day without truffles, and they're by far the biggest item at chocolate festivals. Years ago I ran a little cottage industry called "The Truffle Hound." I spent three months dipping truffles in anticipation of February; perhaps that's why I gave it up. In small batches, chocolate dipping is actually quite therapeutic—but increasing the pace made me feel like I'd stepped into the scene from that classic chocolate factory episode of **I Love Lucy**. In the end, I was dipped in chocolate along with the entire kitchen. That's why I always recommend making truffles in small, manageable quantities. Relax and enjoy the experience!*

1 pound white chocolate almond bark
1 cup (2 sticks) unsalted butter, softened
1/4 cup amaretto liqueur
1 pound white chocolate candy coating*
2 tablespoons butter-flavored shortening
1 cup chopped toasted almonds**

Chop up almond bark so that almonds are in very small pieces. Place in top of double boiler and melt over hot (not boiling) water, making sure that water does not touch bottom of upper pan. Remove chocolate from over water and cool about 10 minutes, stirring occasionally. Cream butter in mixing bowl. Gradually beat in melted chocolate, then liqueur. Cover bowl with plastic wrap and let stand an hour or two until mixture begins to set. Re-whip until light and creamy.

Use a miniature ice cream scoop to shape truffles. Place scoops on foil-covered baking sheet and chill about 1 hour before dipping. For best results, work with a dozen truffles at one time, keeping the rest refrigerated.

Combine white chocolate candy coating and shortening in top of double boiler. Melt over hot (not boiling) water, making sure that water does not touch bottom of upper pan. (When using candy coating, it's particularly important that no droplets of steam come in contact with the coating. This will cause it to "seize," or harden.) Stir until coating is smooth and creamy. Have chopped almonds ready in shallow plate or pie pan. Have a second foil-covered baking sheet ready to receive dipped truffles. Using a long fondue fork or chocolate dipping loop, lift one truffle off foil and quickly slide off fork into melted coating. Lift back out of coating, allowing excess to drip back into pan. Slip truffle off fork and into chopped almonds, coating one side. Lift truffle out of almonds and onto foil. Repeat with remaining truffles. Chill truffles to set. These are best when eaten at room temperature, but should be stored in the refrigerator.

NOTE: Chocolate candy coating is different from regular chocolate or white chocolate: it contains vegetable oil instead of cocoa butter. Cocoa butter requires special tempering to prevent it from forming an unattractive gray "bloom" on the surface of remelted chocolate. For this reason I always buy the best-quality chocolate for my truffle fillings and use the coating for dipping only; the slight difference in taste is hardly noticeable. Look for chocolate candy coating in bags of wafers or chips. They are sold in cake decorating shops and many supermarkets.

**NOTE:* Toast almonds in a 375°F (190°C) oven for 5 to 10 minutes, stirring 3 times while baking.

President's Day Cherry Pie Squares
MAKES 16 SQUARES

❖

It just wouldn't be February without a Monday holiday and cherry pie. Who's observing whom's birthday on which day makes it confusing to go to the bank or the post office. I once had to bring a cherry dessert to a bazaar and was racking my brain for inspiration. Then I noticed him . . . staring back at me from the breakfast table. I don't know who the guy on the Quaker Oats box is supposed to be, but he sure reminds me of George Washington. Anyway, the oatmeal ended up in this recipe.

1/3 cup firmly packed, light brown sugar
1 cup toasted chopped almonds
1 cup quick or old fashioned rolled oats
1/2 cup (1 stick) unsalted butter, softened
3/4 cup all-purpose flour
CHERRY FILLING (recipe follows) or
21-ounce can cherry pie filling

CHERRY FILLING

16-ounce can pitted red tart cherries
1 cup sugar
1/4 cup cornstarch
1 teaspoon almond extract

Preheat oven to 400°F (200°C). In a large mixing bowl combine sugar, almonds, oats, and flour. Cut in butter until mixture is crumbly. Reserve 1 1/2 cups of mixture and press the remainder into a 9-inch square baking dish. Cover with filling and sprinkle with remaining crumbs, pressing lightly onto filling. Bake 20 to 25 minutes, or until lightly browned. Cool completely. Cut into squares.

Drain juice from cherries, reserving all of juice. Combine sugar and cornstarch in a medium saucepan. Blend in cherry juice. Bring to boil over medium heat, stirring constantly until mixture thickens and boils. Stir in cherries. Remove from heat and stir in almond extract. Cool before using in bars.

Opposite: Bell Pepper Jelly, page 31

ST. PATRICK'S DAY SHAMROCK SCONES
MAKES 1 DOZEN

❖

*A*ny *mid-March baking bazaar will be stocked with St. Patrick's Day sweets. It's the "eating of the green," and just about everything has been doused with food dye. That's what's so refreshing about these shamrock-shaped scones. The traditional batter remains its traditional color.*

1³/4 cups all-purpose flour
3 tablespoons sugar
2¹/2 teaspoons baking powder
¹/4 teaspoon salt
¹/3 cup chilled unsalted butter
¹/2 cup dried currants
¹/3 cup chopped toasted almonds*
1 tablespoon grated orange peel
1 egg, beaten with ¹/2 teaspoon
almond extract
4 to 6 tablespoons half-and-half

Combine flour, sugar, baking powder, and salt in medium mixing bowl. Cut in butter until mixture resembles fine crumbs. Stir in currants, almonds, orange peel, egg mixture, and just enough half-and-half to make dough cling together.

Preheat oven to 400°F (200°C). Line baking sheet with parchment. Turn dough out onto lightly floured surface and knead 10 times. Divide into 36 equal balls. Arrange balls in clusters of three, 4 inches apart on prepared baking sheet. Flatten clusters to resemble shamrocks. Bake until golden brown, 8 to 12 minutes. Carefully lift from baking parchment with spatula.

NOTE: Toast almonds in a 375°F (190°C) oven for 5 to 10 minutes, stirring 3 times while baking.

Opposite: Three-Berry Preserves, page 32

EASTER BUNNY BREAD
MAKES 6 LARGE OR 12 SMALL BUNNIES

❖

*B*unny *bread has become a tradition at spring bazaars. It makes an adorable addition to the egg basket on Easter morning. Unlike chocolate rabbits, these are great to eat for breakfast.*

1 cup milk
1/4 cup (1/2 stick) unsalted butter, cut into cubes
1/2 cup warm water (105°F to 115°F/about 45°C)
1/4 cup honey
2 envelopes active dry yeast
5 to 6 cups all-purpose flour
1/2 cup firmly packed dark brown sugar
1 tablespoon cinnamon
1 teaspoon salt
4 eggs, room temperature
1 egg mixed with 1 tablespoon water
ROYAL ICING (recipe follows)
chocolate chips
1/8-inch-wide pastel ribbon (optional decoration)*

Combine milk and butter in small saucepan, and place over low heat until butter melts. Cool to lukewarm (110°F/45°C). Combine warm water and honey in small dish. Stir in yeast. Let stand until foamy, about 5 minutes. Combine 4 cups flour with brown sugar, cinnamon, and salt in large mixing bowl. Add 4 eggs, yeast mixture and milk mixture, and stir to blend. Add enough of

remaining flour to make a soft but not sticky dough. Knead on lightly floured surface (or in electric mixer with dough hook) until smooth and elastic, about 8 to 10 minutes. Place dough in lightly oiled large bowl and turn once to coat with oil. Cover with towel and let rise in warm, draft-free area until doubled in bulk, about 1 1/2 hours.

FOR LARGE BUNNIES

Coat baking sheets with nonstick cooking spray. Divide dough into 6 equal pieces. Working with one piece, mold about 1/2 cup dough into egg shape for bunny body. Place on prepared baking sheet. Break off about 1/4 cup dough from remainder of piece and roll into ball. Dip one edge of ball in water and attach to body for head. Shape remaining dough into 2 long logs (for ears) and 4 short logs (for legs). Dip base of each ear in water and tuck under head. Pinch ends of ears into points. Dip short logs in water and tuck under body for legs. Repeat with remaining dough pieces, making 5 more bunnies. Space bunnies at least 3 inches apart on baking sheet. Cover with towel and let rise in warm, draft free area until doubled in bulk, 30 minutes to 1 hour.

Preheat oven to 350°F (180°C). Uncover bunnies and brush with egg-and-water glaze. Bake until bread is golden brown and sounds hollow when tapped, about 20 minutes. Let cool on wire racks.

FOR SMALL BUNNIES

Follow the same instructions, but begin by dividing dough into 12 equal parts. Bake about 15 minutes.

TO DECORATE

Pipe royal icing through pastry bag to create eyes, nose, and mouth. Use chocolate chips for pupils in eyes. Pipe a row of buttons down the front of each bunny.

ROYAL ICING

1 egg white
$1/4$ teaspoon cream of tartar
$1^1/2$ cups powdered sugar
red food coloring

Combine egg white and cream of tartar in large, greasefree mixing bowl and beat with electric mixer until foamy. Add powdered sugar and beat until icing is stiff, about 5 minutes. Tint pink with food coloring.

NOTE: If desired, tie bows around bunnies' necks using $1/8$-inch pastel satin ribbon.

Hot-Crossed Buns
MAKES 32 BUNS

❖

*M*y childhood memories of Easter bazaars are synonymous with hot-crossed buns. To be honest, I preferred some bakers' versions to others. I never cared much for the weird-looking green citron. This British recipe is more to my liking. The mashed potato dough is spiked with orange peel, currants, candied pineapple, and ginger.

2 packages dry active yeast
1/2 cup warm water (105°F, about 45°C)
1/2 cup lukewarm milk
3/4 cup mashed potatoes (or instant)
1/4 cup sugar
1/4 cup honey
1 teaspoon salt
1/2 cup (1 stick) unsalted butter, softened
2 eggs
1 teaspoon cinnamon
1/2 teaspoon nutmeg
1 cup dried currants
1/2 cup finely chopped candied pineapples
2 tablespoons finely chopped candied ginger
2 tablespoons finely shredded orange peel
4 1/2 cups all-purpose flour
1 egg yolk, beaten with 2 tablespoons of water
VANILLA GLAZE (recipe follows)

In large mixing bowl, dissolve yeast in water. Stir in milk, mashed potatoes, sugar, honey, butter, eggs, cinnamon, nutmeg, currants, pineapple, ginger, orange peel, and 2 1/2 cups flour. Beat until smooth. Mix in remaining flour to form soft dough. Knead dough on lightly floured surface (or in an electric mixer with dough hook) until smooth and elastic, about 5 minutes. Place dough in lightly oiled large bowl and turn once to coat with oil. Cover with towel and let rise in warm draft free area until doubled in bulk, about 1 1/2 hours. Punch down dough and shape into 32 balls. Grease large baking sheet or line with parchment. Place balls 2 inches apart on sheet. With scissors, snip a cross on top of each bun. Cover with towel and let rise in warm, draft-free area until doubled in bulk.

Preheat oven to 375°F (190°C). Brush tops of buns with egg yolk and water mixture. Bake 20 minutes or until golden brown. Cool. Put glaze in a plastic sandwich bag and snip off small opening in lower corner. Pipe icing along cross cuts on buns.

VANILLA GLAZE

1 cup powdered sugar
1 tablespoon milk or half-and-half
1 teaspoon vanilla

Place powdered sugar in small bowl. Add milk, mixing to form a smooth glaze. Flavor with vanilla.

Star-Spangled Berry Tarts
MAKES 1 DOZEN 3-INCH TARTS

❖

These patriotic little pies have a crunchy pecan cookie crust. Accenting the strawberries and blueberries with cream cheese stars reminds one of Old Glory. Don't be deceived—these only look difficult to make. No pie crust to roll. No filling to cook. The important thing is to serve them soon after they've been assembled. But then, these disappear so fast that it shouldn't be a problem!

3 cups all-purpose flour
1/3 cup firmly packed light brown sugar
1 cup (2 sticks) unsalted butter, softened
1 1/2 cups toasted chopped pecans*
1 egg
1 1/2 to 2 cups strawberry or red currant jelly
1 quart fresh strawberries
1 quart fresh blueberries
one 8-ounce and one 3-ounce package cream cheese, softened
1 teaspoon vanilla
2 tablespoons powdered sugar

Preheat oven to 350°F (180°C). Combine flour, brown sugar, butter, pecans, and egg in large mixing bowl and blend by hand or with mixer until soft dough forms. Divide into 12 balls and press firmly and evenly against bottoms and sides of 3-inch false-bottomed tart pans. Bake until golden, 15 to 20 minutes. Cool completely, then remove from pans.

Melt jelly in small saucepan over low heat or in microwave. Brush thin glaze of jelly on inside of tarts. Let set. Pick over strawberries and blueberries, discarding any unattractive fruit. Split strawberries in half. Arrange cut side down, fanning out across half of each tart. Fill remaining half of each tart with blueberries. Remelt jelly, if necessary, and brush over tops of tarts, completely glazing berries. Chill long enough to set jelly.

Beat cream cheese with vanilla and powdered sugar until light and fluffy. Fill pastry bag fitted with medium star tip. Pipe a row of stars down center of each tart between strawberries and blueberries. Chill until ready to serve. These are best when eaten the same day.

NOTE: Toast pecans in a 375°F (190°C) oven for 5 to 10 minutes, stirring 3 times while baking.

FOURTH OF JULY LEMON MERINGUE PIE
MAKES ONE 9-INCH PIE

———— ❖ ————

*L*emon meringue pie is a classic summertime dessert and a July Fourth favorite. This *seasonal popularity has always puzzled me—because ironically, the months that we crave the pie the most are the months it "misbehaves." Anyone who's ever baked a lemon meringue pie will tell you that it's the prima donna of pastries. Mother Nature, in the form of summer heat and humidity, is mostly to blame. Weepy, shrinking meringue is about as predictable as summertime sunburn. No wonder country fair bakers find it the ultimate challenge. Some cooking contests revolve around the "perfect" lemon meringue pie. I've seen many interesting techniques. Some bakers use an egg-and-butter filling resembling English lemon curd. Others focus on making a pie as high as it is wide. I've even seen meringues made with marshmallow fluff. However, tradition usually wins. That's what I like about this recipe: the old-fashioned filling is cooked on the stovetop and covered with an impressive eight-egg-white meringue.*

SOME LEMON MERINGUE PIE POINTERS

- Always spread meringue completely over *warm* filling, sealing around the edges of the crust.
- Use superfine sugar for a smoother-textured meringue that's less likely to become gummy.
- Lemon meringue pie is at its peak when served two hours after baking. If kept overnight, it must be stored in the refrigerator, but the meringue will lose its fresh texture and become slightly rubbery.

COUNTRY CREAM PIE PASTRY (single crust,
page 7) or
EGG AND VINEGAR PIE PASTRY (single crust,
page 8)
1^1/$_2$ cups sugar
3 tablespoons cornstarch
3 tablespoons all-purpose flour
1/8 teaspoon salt
1^1/$_2$ cups water
8 egg yolks (reserve whites for meringue)
1^1/$_2$ teaspoons grated lemon peel
6 tablespoons fresh lemon juice
3 tablespoons unsalted butter
MERINGUE (recipe follows)

Preheat oven to 375°F (190°C). Prepare 9-inch
pie shell as directed in one of the piecrust recipes.
Spray one side of 12-inch square of aluminum foil
with nonstick cooking spray. Line pie shell with
foil, sprayed side down. Fill with dried beans or
pie weights. Bake until set, 15 to 17 minutes.
Remove beans and foil. Continue baking until
golden brown, 5 to 10 minutes. Cool completely.

Combine sugar, cornstarch, flour, and salt in
medium saucepan. Slowly whisk in water. Beat egg
yolks in separate bowl until blended. Bring mixture
in saucepan to boil over medium heat, and cook,
whisking constantly, 3 minutes. Slowly pour about
half of mixture into egg yolks, and whisk until
smooth. Pour yolk mixture back into saucepan and
cook 3 minutes longer, whisking constantly. Add
lemon peel, juice, and butter and cook over low
heat 2 minutes, stirring with rubber spatula and

scraping along bottom of pan to prevent mixture
from sticking and burning. Cool filling about 10
minutes while preparing meringue.

MERINGUE

8 egg whites, room temperature
1/2 teaspoon cream of tartar
1 cup superfine sugar
1 teaspoon vanilla

Preheat oven to 350°F (180°C). Combine egg
whites and cream of tartar in clean, greasefree
mixing bowl and beat with electric mixer until
soft peaks barely begin to form. Gradually beat
in sugar, adding vanilla with the last spoonful.
Continue beating until meringue holds glossy
peaks.

Pour warm lemon filling into cooled pie shell.
Spread meringue over filling, covering completely
and sealing to edges. Heap extra meringue high in
center of pie, spreading with peaks and swirls.
Bake 15 minutes. Let cool 2 hours before serving.

COLONIAL TOMBSTONE COOKIES
MAKES 1 TO 1¹/2 DOZEN COOKIES

❖

This concept occurred to me when I was asked to bake cookies for an Octoberfest. Actually, these work as well for the Fourth of July as they do for Halloween. The idea came from an old cemetery that I pass frequently. One day I spotted a class of grade-school children doing crayon-and-paper rubbings of the old headstones in the graveyard. I stopped to examine some myself. It was amazing how many dated back to the seventeenth and eighteenth centuries. Then it occurred to me, why not bake cookies in the shape of headstones? For names and dates I used Pilgrims, patriots, and presidents. In case you don't have a set of encyclopedias in your kitchen, I've included a dozen names and dates at the end of the recipe.

1/2 cup butter-flavored shortening
1/4 cup (1/2 stick) unsalted butter
1 cup firmly packed dark brown sugar
2 eggs
1 teaspoon vanilla
2 1/2 cups all-purpose flour
1 teaspoon baking powder
1/2 teaspoon salt
coconut
green food coloring
CHOCOLATE ICING (recipe follows)

Cream shortening, butter, and brown sugar in large mixing bowl until fluffy. Beat in eggs and vanilla. Combine flour, baking powder, and salt in separate bowl, and blend into egg mixture to form smooth dough. Divide in half and wrap in plastic. Chill at least 2 hours. Cut cookie pattern from cardboard: tombstone should be about 3 × 6 inches and rounded at the top.

Preheat oven to 400°F (200°C). Line baking sheets with parchment. For best results, use lightly floured pastry cloth with rolling pin cover. Work with half of dough at a time, keeping remainder refrigerated. Roll dough out to about 1/8 inch thick. Place cardboard pattern on dough and cut around it, using sturdy sewing needle. Arrange cookies on prepared baking sheets. Bake until cookies are set and lightly golden, 6 to 8 minutes. Cool on parchment, then lift gently with spatula.

Opposite: Spiced Grape Jam, page 33

Combine coconut and a few drops green food coloring in jar and shake until coconut is evenly tinted. Spread a thin band of chocolate icing along base of each tombstone. Cover chocolate with coconut to resemble grass. Using small pastry bag fitted with fine writing tip, pipe name and dates on each tombstone.

CHOCOLATE ICING

1¹/₂ cups powdered sugar
¹/₄ cup Dutch-process cocoa
3 to 5 tablespoons light cream or
half-and-half

Combine powdered sugar and cocoa in mixing bowl. Add enough cream to make a smooth glaze.

NAMES AND DATES OF FOUNDING FATHERS (AND MOTHERS)

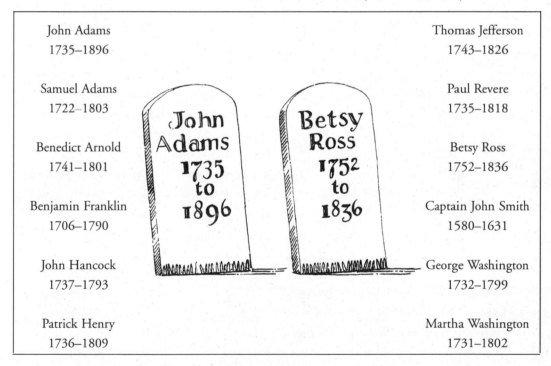

John Adams
1735–1896

Samuel Adams
1722–1803

Benedict Arnold
1741–1801

Benjamin Franklin
1706–1790

John Hancock
1737–1793

Patrick Henry
1736–1809

Thomas Jefferson
1743–1826

Paul Revere
1735–1818

Betsy Ross
1752–1836

Captain John Smith
1580–1631

George Washington
1732–1799

Martha Washington
1731–1802

Opposite: Green Apple Chutney, page 35

CRANBERRY PUMPKIN BREAD
MAKES TWO 9 × 5 × 3-INCH LOAVES

❖

Cream cheese gives this bread a texture resembling pound cake. I've bought and sold many loaves of pumpkin bread at pumpkin festivals and I still think this version is special. You can serve it for breakfast on Thanksgiving morning, then turn around, top it with ice cream and serve it for dessert!

8-ounce package cream cheese, softened
1/2 cup (1 stick) unsalted butter, softened
1 1/2 cups granulated sugar
1 cup firmly packed dark brown sugar
4 eggs
2 cups oven-baked pumpkin or one
16-ounce can solid-pack pumpkin*
3 1/2 cups all-purpose flour
2 teaspoons baking soda
1/2 teaspoon baking powder
1/2 teaspoon salt
1 teaspoon cinnamon
1/2 teaspoon nutmeg
1/2 teaspoon ginger
1/4 teaspoon ground cloves
1 cup chopped toasted walnuts**
1 cup fresh cranberries, chopped

Preheat oven to 350°F (180°C). Grease bottoms only of two 9 × 5 × 3-inch loaf pans or line with baking parchment. (If using disposable foil pans, simply coat bottoms with nonstick cooking spray.) Beat cream cheese, butter, and sugars together until light and fluffy. Beat in eggs one at a time, blending well after each addition. Blend in pumpkin. Combine flour, baking soda, baking powder, salt, and spices in separate bowl. Add to pumpkin mixture along with walnuts and cranberries, mixing just until all ingredients are moistened. Divide batter between pans and bake until toothpick inserted in center comes out clean, about 1 hour. Cool 5 minutes, then remove from pans and cool completely on racks. (If using foil pans, cool bread in pans.) Keep tightly wrapped and store in refrigerator for easier slicing.

NOTE: To bake pumpkin, split one medium pumpkin into quarters. Discard pulp and seeds. Arrange pieces in roasting pan, cover with foil, and bake at 375°F (190°C) until flesh is very tender and much of the moisture has evaporated, 1¹/4 to 1¹/2 hours. Peel pumpkin and purée in processor until very smooth. Measure 2 cups purée; reserve any remainder for another use.

**NOTE:* Toast walnuts in a 375°F (190°C) oven for 5 to 10 minutes, stirring 3 times while baking.

SHAKER SUGAR-PUMPKIN PIE
MAKES ONE 9-INCH PIE

❖

*P*umpkin festivals are a favorite autumn event. This is particularly true in the New England states, where the pumpkin is a revered symbol of our colonial heritage. At one of these autumn fests you can sample pumpkin cooked in every possible form, from pumpkin stew to pumpkin pancakes. Of course, pumpkin pie is the all-time favorite. Leftover Jack O'Lanterns are not the preferred pumpkin for pies. Small, sweet pumpkins known as "sugar" pumpkins traditionally make the very best pies. For an authentic colonial flavor, try baking this in a cornmeal pastry crust.

2^1/2 to 3 pound sugar pumpkin (or one 16-ounce can solid-pack pumpkin)
^{1}/2 cup firmly packed dark brown sugar
^{1}/2 cup molasses or maple syrup
1 teaspoon cinnamon
^{1}/2 teaspoon ground ginger
1^1/4 teaspoons nutmeg
1^1/4 teaspoons ground cloves
2 eggs
1 cup heavy cream
CORNMEAL PASTRY CRUST AND PASTRY PUMPKIN (recipe follows)

Preheat oven to 400°F (200°C). Cover jelly roll pan with foil and place pumpkin in center. Pierce pumpkin about a dozen times with fork. Bake until flesh is tender and most of the moisture has evaporated, 1 to 1^1/2 hours. Cool. Split pumpkin in half and discard seeds. Measure out about 2^1/2 cups pulp, place in a mixing bowl, and mash with mixer or potato masher. Blend in brown sugar,

molasses, and spices. Beat in eggs and cream. Pour into prepared pie shell.

Preheat oven again, this time to 425°F (220°C). Place pie on baking sheet in bottom third of oven. Bake 15 minutes. Reduce heat to 350°F (180°C) and bake 20 minutes longer. Move pie to center of oven and continue baking until filling is set, another 25 to 30 minutes. Cool. Garnish pie with baked pastry pumpkin.

CORNMEAL PASTRY CRUST AND PASTRY PUMPKIN
MAKES ONE 9-INCH PIE SHELL

❖

1 cup all-purpose flour
^{1}/$_4$ cup yellow cornmeal
^{1}/$_2$ teaspoon salt
6 tablespoons butter-flavored shortening
5 to 6 tablespoons apple cider
1 egg beaten with 2 tablespoons water

Combine flour, cornmeal, and salt in bowl. Cut in shortening until mixture resembles small peas. Gradually add cider, tossing lightly with fork; add just enough so that dough clings together in ball. For best results, use lightly floured pastry cloth with rolling pin cover. Roll pastry into a 12-inch circle. Ease into 9-inch pie pan. Trim edges a ^{1}/$_2$-inch overhang and crimp. Reserve trimmings.

For pastry pumpkin, gather dough scraps together and roll out into about a 4 × 6-inch oval. Trim into shape of pumpkin with stem. Score sections of pumpkin with knife. Brush with egg mixture to glaze.

Preheat oven to 400°F (200°C). Bake pie shell and pastry pumpkin until golden, 8 to 10 minutes. Let cool before filling pie shell.

SNOWMEN MERINGUES
MAKES 1 DOZEN

✦

Meringue kisses are traditional holiday bazaar confections. They're somewhere in between a cookie and a candy, and lighten up a dessert tray like delicate snowflakes. It was only inevitable that these would eventually evolve into snowmen. Now you see them everywhere; it just wouldn't be a Christmas bazaar without snowmen meringues. No wonder they're so popular—children adore them, and they're a delightful addition to a dish of ice cream.

2 egg whites, room temperature
1/8 teaspoon cream of tartar
1/2 cup sugar
dried currants
a few pieces of candied orange peel

Heat oven to 200°F (130°C). Line large baking sheet with parchment. Combine egg whites and cream of tartar in clean, grease-free mixing bowl and beat with electric mixer until soft peaks form. Gradually add 1/4 cup sugar, beating until meringue is stiff and glossy. Gently fold in remaining 1/4 cup sugar with wire whisk. Spoon meringue into pastry bag fitted with large round nozzle. Pipe each snowman as a series of 3 connecting circles: 2 1/2-inch diameter for the base, 2-inch for the midsection, and 1-inch for the head. Snowmen should be at least 2 1/2 inches apart. Cut currants into very small pieces. Cut orange peel into 1/2-inch long thick, wedgelike slivers resembling tiny carrots. Use pieces of currant for eyes, a smiling upturned mouth and buttons, just as you'd use coals on a real snowman. Position orange peel as if it were a carrot nose. Bake 1 1/2 hours. Turn off heat and leave meringues in oven 2 hours longer. Cool slightly, then transfer meringues to tightly covered container.

NOTE: Ovens vary dramatically when you start baking in the 200°F (130°C) range. Electric ovens, in particular, may cycle on and off. I've lived in four different houses with four different ovens. Each time I moved, I had to adjust my meringue recipes. Experiment! You may have to turn the temperature to 225°F or 250°F (140°C or 155°C), or bake them for a longer or shorter period of time. Always start out low, because once you brown meringues, you can't make them white again.

HELPFUL HINT: Meringues can get chewy within minutes of contact with humidity. That's why it's important to store them while they are still barely warm but have hardened. The best way to sell these at bazaars or give them as gifts is individually wrapped. Slip meringues into sandwich bags and tie tops tightly with pieces of ribbon. Once again, it's important to do this while they're fairly fresh from the oven but cool enough to handle.

CHOCOLATE PEPPERMINT PINWHEELS
MAKES 5 DOZEN

❖

These cookies have special memories for me. I remember the ritual of baking them for the holidays. Mom would roll out the dough and I would smash up the peppermint candies. Whenever she turned away, I would sprinkle some of the sugary dust into my mouth; sometimes there wasn't enough left for the cookies! We used to thread these with ribbons to sell as ornaments at the church bazaar. We once tried to hang them all over our own tree, but they disappeared before Christmas!

1 cup (2 sticks) unsalted butter, softened
1 cup powdered sugar
1/2 to 1 teaspoon peppermint extract
2 1/2 cups all-purpose flour
1/4 teaspoon salt
1/4 cup Dutch-process cocoa
3/4 cup crushed peppermint candies
red food coloring
thin plastic straw
thin ribbon or cord

Cream butter with powdered sugar in mixing bowl. Blend in peppermint extract, flour, and salt. Divide dough in half. Blend cocoa into one half of dough. Blend 2 tablespoons crushed peppermints into other half. Tint peppermint dough with red food coloring until light pink. Wrap the doughs separately and chill at least 2 hours.

For best results, use lightly floured pastry cloth with rolling pin cover. Roll out chocolate dough into 10 × 15-inch rectangle about 1/8 inch thick. Place on sheet of plastic wrap or waxed paper. Roll out pink dough to exactly the same size. Place pink dough on top of chocolate dough. Roll layers up together, jelly roll fashion, into 15-inch log. Wrap log and chill two hours.

Preheat oven to 400°F (200°C). Cut log into even 1/4-inch slices. Arrange 1 inch apart on baking sheet lined with parchment. Sprinkle cookies lightly with remaining crushed peppermint candy. Use small plastic straw to pierce hole about 1/4 inch from edge of each cookie. Bake until cookies are set and tinged with pale gold, 10 to 14 minutes. While cookies are hot, re-pierce each hole with the straw. Cool cookies and lift from parchment with spatula. Cut 7-inch lengths of ribbon or cord. String through cookies and tie into loops.

Opposite: Chocolate Cherry Sweethearts With Almond Icing, page 41

Gingerbread Teddy Bears
MAKES 2 TO 3 DOZEN

❖

Gingerbread bears are lovable and surprisingly simple to make. All you need is a traditional gingerbread boy cookie cutter, some scraps of dough, and some raisins. People buy these by the dozen at holiday bazaars just to decorate their homes (I like to line mine up across the fireplace mantel). They also make adorable stocking stuffers.

$^{1}/_{2}$ cup (1 stick) unsalted butter, softened
$^{1}/_{2}$ cup butter-flavored shortening
1 cup dark molasses
3 cups all-purpose flour
2 teaspoons baking soda
1 teaspoon salt
$^{1}/_{2}$ teaspoon ground ginger
$^{1}/_{2}$ teaspoon cinnamon
$^{1}/_{4}$ teaspoon nutmeg
$^{1}/_{4}$ teaspoon ground cloves
raisins

Cream butter and shortening in large mixing bowl. Blend in molasses. Combine flour, baking soda, salt, and spices in separate bowl. Add to molasses mixture, mixing to form smooth dough. Divide into 3 parts and wrap in plastic. Chill several hours.

For best results, use lightly floured pastry cloth with rolling pin cover. Work with $^{1}/_{3}$ of dough at a time, keeping remainder refrigerated. Roll dough out to about $^{1}/_{8}$ inch thick. Cut with 5-inch gingerbread boy cookie cutter. (Don't use cutters with pointed heads or hats.) Place cookies 3 inches apart on baking sheets lined with parchment. Use scraps of dough to mold little balls about the size of ears and a muzzle. Press an ear against each side of head and flatten with finger. (Ears should look bearlike, not mouselike.) Place another ball in center of head for a muzzle, and press raisin into center for nose. Cut a raisin in half and use for eyes.

Preheat oven to 350°F (180°C). When all the bears have ears and faces, bake until set and lightly golden, 8 to 10 minutes. Cool on baking parchment, then gently lift off with spatula.

Opposite: Easter Bunny Bread
With Royal Icing, page 46

Candy Cane Coffee Cakes
MAKES 3 COFFEE CAKES

❖

Candy cane coffee cake was a Christmas morning tradition at my house. Some years we'd bake one; other years we'd buy one from the church bazaar. Everybody seemed to bake them. The fillings varied, but the delicious sour cream dough was always the same. I still see those cane-shaped coffee cakes showing up at holiday sales, and I can't leave without taking one home.

2 envelopes active dry yeast
1/2 cup warm water (105°F to 115°F/75°C)
1 pint (16 ounces) sour cream
1/4 cup (1/2 stick) unsalted butter, softened
1/3 cup sugar
2 teaspoons salt
1 teaspoon almond extract
2 eggs, room temperature
51/2 to 6 cups all-purpose flour
FRUIT AND NUT FILLING (recipe follows)
3 tablespoons unsalted butter, melted
ALMOND GLAZE (recipe follows)
red candied cherries and green
candied pineapple

Dissolve yeast in warm water in large mixing bowl. Heat sour cream in saucepan over very low heat or in microwave, until lukewarm. Add to yeast mixture. Beat in butter, sugar, salt, almond extract, eggs, and 2 cups flour until smooth. Mix in enough of remaining flour to make an easy-to-handle dough. Knead dough on floured surface (or in electric mixer with dough hook attachment) until smooth and elastic, about 10 minutes. Place in large oiled bowl and turn to coat all sides with oil. Cover with plastic wrap and let rise in warm, draft-free area until doubled in bulk, about 1 hour.

Preheat oven to 375°F (190°C). Punch down dough and divide into 3 equal parts. For best results, use lightly floured pastry cloth with rolling pin cover. Roll each third of dough into a 6 × 15-inch rectangle. Transfer to 3 baking sheets lined with baking parchment. Cut along sides of each rectangle with scissors, making 2-inch deep cuts at 1/2-inch intervals (Fig. 1). Divide filling into 3 parts and spread down center of each rectangle.

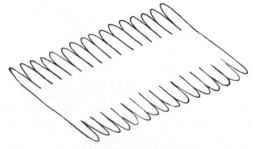

Fig. 1

Criss-cross strips over filling (Fig. 2).

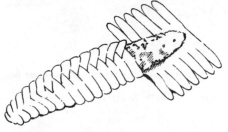

Fig. 2

Stretch dough another 7 inches, bending to form a cane (Fig. 3). Bake each coffee cake until golden brown, 15 to 20 minutes. (Keep unbaked coffee cakes, waiting for the oven, in refrigerator to

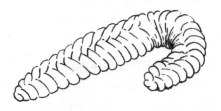

Fig. 3

prevent rising.) Brush with melted butter and drizzle with glaze. Decorate with halves of red cherries and thin-sliced green pineapple wedges for leaves (Fig. 4).

Fig. 4

FRUIT AND NUT FILLING

1 cup maraschino (not candied) cherries, well drained and chopped
1/2 cup candied pineapple, chopped
1/2 cup golden raisins
1/2 cup pitted dates, chopped
1/2 cup chopped toasted almonds*
2 tablespoons apricot jam

Mix fruits and almonds together in bowl. Toss with apricot jam to moisten.

NOTE: Toast almonds in a 375°F (190°C) oven for 5 to 10 minutes, stirring 3 times while baking.

ALMOND GLAZE

2 cups powdered sugar
2 to 3 tablespoons milk
1/2 teaspoon almond extract

Place powdered sugar in small mixing bowl. Add enough milk to make smooth glaze. Flavor with almond extract.

CHRISTMAS CHEESECAKE
MAKES ONE 9-INCH CAKE

❖

This cheesecake tastes like a cross between eggnog and rum-raisin ice cream. It's a great holiday dessert and a fast-selling favorite at bazaars. I always have to bake several.

1 cup rolled oats
1/4 cup chopped toasted pecans*
3 tablespoons unsalted butter, melted
3 tablespoons firmly packed light brown sugar
two 8-ounce packages cream cheese, softened
1/3 cup granulated sugar
2 tablespoons all-purpose flour
2 eggs
1/2 cup sour cream
1/4 teaspoon nutmeg
1/3 cup golden raisins soaked overnight
in 3 tablespoons rum
RAISIN-NUT TOPPING (recipe follows)

Preheat oven to 350°F (180°C). Combine oats, pecans, butter, and brown sugar in small mixing bowl. Press onto bottom of 9-inch springform pan. Bake 15 minutes. Keep oven on.

Beat cream cheese, sugar, and flour in large mixing bowl with electric mixer until smooth. Add eggs one at a time, mixing well after each addition. Blend in sour cream and nutmeg. Stir in raisins and rum. Pour over crust; sprinkle with topping. Bake 50 minutes. Run spatula around rim of pan to loosen cake. Cool completely before removing rim of pan. Store cheesecake in refrigerator.

RAISIN-NUT TOPPING

2 tablespoons rolled oats
2 tablespoons all-purpose flour
1/3 cup firmly packed light brown sugar
2 tablespoons unsalted butter, softened
1/4 cup chopped toasted pecans**
1/3 cup golden raisins

Combine oatmeal, flour, and brown sugar in small mixing bowl. Cut in butter until mixture is crumbly. Stir in pecans and raisins.

*NOTE: Toast pecans in a 375°F (290°C) oven for 5 to 10 minutes, stirring 3 times while baking.

**HELPFUL HINT: If you're taking this cheesecake to a bazaar, you don't want to sell the bottom of your springform pan along with it! I always cut a 9-inch round of baking parchment to fit the bottom of my pan. Once the cheesecake is chilled, it's easy to run a spatula under the paper and transfer the cake to a tray or box. You can also bake this in a 9-inch round disposable aluminum cake pan that comes with a plastic cover.

PISTACHIO-ALMOND CAKE
MAKES ONE 8-INCH CAKE

❖

If you're looking for an all-purpose holiday cake to take you through the season, this is the one. It's easy to bake and exquisite when glazed with chocolate or simply dusted with powdered sugar. I serve it at home with puréed raspberries.

3/4 cup sugar
1/2 cup (1 stick) unsalted butter, softened
8-ounce can or package of almond paste
3 eggs
1 tablespoon Triple Sec
1/4 teaspoon almond extract
a few drops green food coloring
1/4 cup all-purpose flour
1/3 teaspoon baking powder
1/2 cup plus 2 tablespoons chopped *unsalted* green pistachios
CHOCOLATE GLAZE (recipe follows) or powdered sugar

Preheat oven to 350°F (180°C). Generously grease and flour a 9-inch springform pan. Combine sugar, butter, and almond paste in a large mixing bowl. Cream together until blended. Beat in eggs, one at a time. Blend in Triple Sec, almond extract, and enough food coloring to tint batter a pale shade of green. Combine flour with baking powder in a separate cup. Add to batter, beating just until blended. Do not over beat. Stir in 1/2 cup pistachios. Pour batter into prepared pan and bake 40 to 45 minutes, or until cake is golden and set in the center. Cool completely. Run a spatula around sides and remove springform. Invert cake onto a platter and remove base. Spread top and sides with a thin layer of chocolate glaze, or place a cake rack over top and dust with powdered sugar (rack will leave grid marks). Sprinkle top of either version with reserved 2 tablespoons of chopped pistachios.

CHOCOLATE GLAZE

---

1 tablespoon butter flavored shortening
1 tablespoon light corn syrup
4-ounce bar dark sweet chocolate

Combine shortening and corn syrup in the top of a double boiler over hot (not boiling) water. Break up chocolate and add to mixture. Stir until glaze is smooth and melted.

Fruitcake Hater's Conversion Cake
Makes Two 9 × 5 × 3-Inch Loaves

❖

We've all heard it a hundred times . . . *"The same fruitcakes just get recycled year after year."* The theory, of course, is that everyone hates fruitcake and would never buy it, much less take the trouble to bake it. As Christmas gifts go, it's become the brunt of practical jokes. Too bad that most people have never really tasted a good fruitcake. One bite from a bad one will sour you on ever giving fruitcake a second chance. Bitter citron is mainly to blame for this undeserved reputation. But fortunately the fruitcake still reigns supreme at holiday bazaars. You'll find the finest examples in the Southern states, where citron is simply not a part of the "fruitcake culture." There you will find buttery cakes filled with roasted pecans, sweet pineapple, cherries, apricots, even pears!

3 cups all-purpose flour
1 1/4 cups firmly packed dark brown sugar
1 1/2 teaspoons baking powder
1/2 teaspoon salt
3/4 cup (1 1/2 sticks) unsalted butter, softened
3/4 cup butter-flavored shortening
9 eggs
1/3 cup orange juice
1/3 cup sherry
1 pound candied pineapple, cubed
8 ounces red candied cherries, halved
4 ounces green candied cherries, halved
8 ounces dried apricots, chopped
8 ounces dried pears or dates, chopped*
8 ounces golden raisins
4 cups toasted pecans**
1/4 cup apricot jam
pecan halves and candied cherried
(optional garnish)

Preheat oven to 275°F (135°C). Coat bottoms only of two 9 × 5 × 3-inch foil loaf pans with nonstick cooking spray. Combine flour, brown sugar, baking powder, salt, butter, shortening, eggs, orange juice, and sherry in large mixing bowl and beat at medium speed until blended. Scrape bowl and beat at high speed 1 minute. Scrap bowl again and beat at high speed 2 minutes longer.

Combine fruits and pecans in 6-quart bowl. Pour batter over fruit mixture and mix gently by hand until blended. Spoon into prepared pans and bake until toothpick inserted in center comes out clean, 2 1/2 to 3 hours.

Transfer cakes to cooling racks. Bring apricot jam to boil. Remove from heat and brush over cakes. If desired, decorate with pecan halves and cherries. Wrap cooled cakes in cellophane or store in airtight containers; chill for easier slicing.

NOTE: When using dried apricots and pears, cover with boiling water and let stand 5 to 10 minutes. Drain well and pat dry with paper towel before adding to batter.

**NOTE:* Toast pecans in a 375°F (190°C) oven for 5 to 10 minutes, stirring 3 times while baking.

HELPFUL HINT: I never use anything but disposable foil pans for fruitcakes, as the cakes can be difficult to remove from regular loaf pans. Decorated gift pans frequently come with their own lids. If you want to remove fruitcakes from foil pans, chill first and flex sides away from cake before inverting. You can even trim the foil away with scissors. Do not invert cakes that have been glazed.

Opposite: Star-Spangled Berry Tarts, page 49
Next page: Colonial Tombstone Cookies With
Chocolate Icing, page 52

Patrick
John
John Adams
1735
1896
Paul Revere
1735
1896
Betsy Ross
1752

Food Festivals, Community Dinners, and Pancake Breakfasts

❖

Winter, spring, summer, and fall, there's always something cooking in a big communal pot. If you've ever been to a pig roast, crab carnival, or lobster fest, you've experienced the essence of America. Food festivals of all types typically reflect regional tastes and flavors. The richly diverse themes all share a common thread: the celebration of nature's bounty.

There are perhaps as many types of festivals as there are favorite foods. From catfish to corn, oysters to oranges, and pork to pumpkins, the events are too numerous to list. This book touches just the tip of the iceberg. Food festivals are not even unique to "country" settings; any area with a colorful local cuisine has every excuse to throw a big bash and invite the public.

The attraction of home cooking doesn't end with the annual festivals and fade away till the following year—far from it. Look around and you'll see great food being dished up by all kinds of organizations for all kinds of causes. Community dinners sponsored by schools, churches and firehouses are one of the most popular means of fund raising. In most cases the kitchen facilities of the institution involved are requisitioned for the meal, but much of the preparation may be done by volunteers on a "potluck" basis. That's not to say that everyone does his or her own thing and shows up with bean casseroles and desserts. The more successful events are known for a specific menu that people come to expect. A committee, knowledgeable about local culinary talent, determines the best recipes and divides the cooking among recruits. As a result, a great deal of pride and personal reputation goes into every chili supper or pancake breakfast.

The recipes in this chapter would normally be served to hungry crowds of hundreds. Obviously they had to be scaled down for the average gathering. I think a yield of eight servings is just about right. After all, you wouldn't prepare such special fare just for yourself; share it with family and friends. Have your own festival!

Food Festivals, Community Dinners, and Pancake Breakfasts

❖

Country Fair Chicken Dinner

Pig Roast

Crab Carnival

Firehouse Chicken Barbecue

Lobster Fest

Church Chili Supper

Pancake Breakfast

COUNTRY FAIR CHICKEN DINNER

❖

Pan-fried chicken is a true delicacy and rapidly becoming a lost treasure. Between fast-food chains, with their pressure fryers, and Shake & Bake®, few people remember how to make the real thing. Furthermore, fried has become the first five-letter "four-letter" word in our language! Fear of frying is a justifiable concern. Hot oil has its hazards, but so do barbecue grills. One should always exercise common sense and caution with either cooking method. As for the fat phobia, all I can say is . . . lighten up your attitude. Leave this classic alone. It's as much a seasonal treat as Thanksgiving turkey with all the trimmings. Besides, when chicken is properly fried and drained, it can be less greasy than some oven-baked versions that are basted in butter or oil to simulate frying. Once you've tasted true fried chicken with pan gravy, mashed potatoes and buttermilk biscuits, you'll appreciate this heirloom of our American culture.

Country Fair Chicken Dinner

❖

Country-Crust Fried Chicken With Creamy Pan Gravy

Parsley Mashed Potatoes and Parsnips

Buttermilk-Bacon Biscuits With Honey Butter

Summer Bean Salad

Strawberry Cream Biscuit Shortcakes

Old Fashioned Pink Lemonade

Country-Crust Fried Chicken With Creamy Pan Gravy
Makes 4 servings (use a second skillet if doubling recipe for 8)

❖

*T*he most popular type of fried chicken is actually prepared "Maryland style"—this means that it's dredged in seasoned flour twice, with an egg wash in between. The result is a flaky crust that can't be matched by other methods.

2 cups all-purpose flour
4 teaspoons paprika
2 teaspoons celery salt
2 teaspoons onion powder
2 teaspoons dried thyme
1 teaspoon dried sage
1/2 teaspoon cracked black pepper
21/2-pound broiler/fryer, cut up
2 eggs
1/2 cup buttermilk
corn oil for frying
Creamy Pan Gravy (recipe follows)

Combine flour and seasonings in large mixing bowl; reserve about 1/4 cup flour mixture for gravy. Blend eggs and buttermilk in separate, shallow bowl. Dredge each piece of chicken in seasoned flour. Dip into egg wash, then recoat with flour mixture. (It helps to use a different hand for each step or else you'll wind up with a sticky coating of flour on your fingertips.) Fill a large, deep skillet with 1 to 11/2 inches of corn oil and heat to 350°F (180°C). (Always use a large burner at the back of your stove to distance yourself from spatter.) Place chicken in oil with tongs and brown lightly on all sides. Reduce heat, cover, and cook for 20 minutes. Turn chicken again and cook uncovered until crust is crisp, 10 to 15 more minutes. Drain well on paper towels.

Heat oven to 100°F (40°C). Transfer chicken to roasting pan lined with more paper towels and keep warm in oven while preparing gravy.

CREAMY PAN GRAVY

❖

Traditionally, pan gravy is made by pouring off all but a trace of the oil and browned bits of flour from the skillet. The gravy is then whipped up in the same pan. This has its drawbacks if doubling a recipe or cooking several batches of chicken. I learned an interesting technique from an old chicken-frying pro: A separate saucepan is used for the gravy. A small amount of pan drippings is spooned out of the skillet and into the saucepan. This also helps keep out any overbrowned crumbs that might be burnt onto the bottom of the skillet.

3 tablespoons chicken drippings (with some bits of browned crust)
1 tablespoon unsalted butter
1/4 cup reserved seasoned flour
2 cups milk
1/2 cup strong chicken broth
pinch each of celery salt and cracked black pepper to taste (optional)

Combine chicken drippings and butter in large saucepan. Add flour and cook over medium heat, stirring constantly, until smooth and bubbly. Slowly blend in milk and chicken broth, and cook, stirring constantly, until gravy is smooth and thickened. Taste and adjust seasoning with celery salt, pepper, and/or your favorite fresh herbs. (Although it's not traditional, I frequently use crushed rosemary.)

PARSLEY MASHED POTATOES AND PARSNIPS
MAKES 8 SERVINGS

❖

*O*nce *I tried these mashed potatoes, I knew there was something special about the recipe. Flecks of fresh parsley and chives were whipped in, along with parsnips. The practice of mashing other vegetables with potatoes apparently dates back to colonial times.*

2 pounds boiling potatoes
1 pound parsnips
5 tablespoons unsalted butter
3/4 to 1 cup buttermilk, warmed
1/4 cup minced fresh parsley
1/4 cup minced fresh chives
1/2 teaspoon salt
1/2 teaspoon cracked black pepper

Peel potatoes and cut into 1-inch cubes. Scrape parsnips and slice into 1/2-inch rounds. Combine potatoes and parsnips in large saucepan, cover with water, and bring to boil. Cook 20 to 25 minutes or until fork-tender. Drain potatoes and parsnips in colander. Melt butter in same saucepan and return potatoes and parsnips. Mash with hand-held potato masher, slowly blending in enough buttermilk to make mixture light and fluffy. Blend in parsley and chives. Season with salt and pepper.

Buttermilk-Bacon Biscuits With Honey Butter
makes 8 biscuits

❖

Some people have been known to pass by mashed potatoes just so they could soak their biscuits in gravy. Others prefer these with honey butter. I like them both ways!

2 cups all-purpose flour
1 tablespoon sugar
2 teaspoons baking powder
1/4 teaspoon baking soda
1/2 teaspoon salt
2 tablespoons crumbled, crisply cooked bacon
1/4 cup butter-flavored shortening
about 3/4 cup buttermilk
Honey Butter (recipe follows)

Honey Butter

2/3 cup unsalted butter, softened
1/3 cup honey

Cream butter with honey, using wire whisk or electric mixer, until mixture is light and fluffy.

Preheat oven to 450°F (230°C). Line baking sheet with parchment. Combine flour, sugar, baking powder, baking soda, salt, and bacon in medium bowl. Cut in shortening until mixture resembles fine crumbs. Using fork, stir in just enough buttermilk to make a dough that clings together. Knead dough about 25 times on lightly floured surface. Pat dough to 1/2-inch thickness and cut with 3-inch biscuit cutter. Arrange biscuits on prepared baking sheet and bake until golden brown, 10 to 12 minutes. Serve warm.

Summer Bean Salad
makes 8 servings

❖

Somewhere, someone must have written down the rule that you can't serve fried chicken without green beans. It seems I've had beans at every chicken dinner since childhood. Green beans have changed a lot over the years. They used to be cooked with bacon for hours, and they always looked awful—limp and khaki-colored. Then people went to the other extreme, serving the beans barely blanched. They remained beautifully green but basically blah. Green beans are one vegetable that really lacks character when eaten almost raw. Somewhere there's a happy medium between crunchy and mushy; beans should be cooked until they're tender enough for the flavor to come through. I like my beans best in a summer salad, tossed with lemon-and-egg dressing. It's the perfect sidekick for fried chicken.

2 pounds fresh green beans
or
1 pound fresh green beans and 1 pound fresh wax beans
1 small red onion, sliced paper-thin
Lemon-And-Egg Dressing (recipe follows)

Remove strings from beans and place beans in very large saucepan. Cover with water and bring to boil. Boil until tender, 10 to 12 minutes (green beans should still be bright green). Immediately drain beans and plunge into large bowl of cold water. Drain beans in a colander. Toss with onion and dressing. Cover and chill at least 3 hours to blend flavors.

Lemon and Egg Dressing

5 tablespoons fresh lemon juice
1 tablespoon sugar
1/2 teaspoon salt
1/4 teaspoon cracked black pepper
3/4 cup vegetable oil
1 tablespoon minced fresh thyme
1 hard-cooked egg, finely chopped

Combine all ingredients in small bowl and whisk to blend.

Strawberry Cream Biscuit Shortcakes
MAKES 8 SERVINGS

❖

These are different from the often heavy baking powder biscuits usually served for strawberry shortcake. This simple pastry has no more than four ingredients, yet it magically bakes into fragile, flaky wafers.

---

1 cup (2 sticks) unsalted butter, softened
1/3 cup heavy cream
2 cups all-purpose flour
granulated sugar
STRAWBERRY FILLING (recipe follows)
COUNTRY CREAM (recipe follows)

Line baking sheets with parchment. Combine butter, cream, and flour in mixing bowl and blend with electric mixer or by hand until soft dough forms. Chill at least 2 hours. For best results use lightly floured pastry cloth with rolling pin cover. Roll out dough to 1/4-inch thickness. Cut with 4-inch biscuit cutter and arrange on prepared baking sheets.

Preheat oven to 375°F (180°C). Prick each biscuit 6 times with fork and sprinkle with sugar. Bake until puffy and crisp, 8 to 10 minutes. Cool on racks. Store in airtight container until ready to assemble shortcakes.

For each shortcake, place one biscuit on plate and top with about 3/4 cup strawberry filling.

Cover with a second biscuit and top it all with about 1/4 cup country cream.

STRAWBERRY FILLING

---

2 quarts fresh strawberries, sliced
3/4 cup superfine sugar
1/4 cup currant jelly, melted

Toss strawberries with sugar and jelly.

COUNTRY CREAM

---

1 1/3 cups chilled heavy cream
1/3 cup sour cream
1/4 cup superfine sugar
1 teaspoon vanilla

Whip heavy cream in large mixing bowl until stiff peaks form. Blend sour cream, sugar, and vanilla in separate dish. Gently fold into whipped cream with rubber spatula.

OLD FASHIONED PINK LEMONADE
MAKES 3^1/2 QUARTS

———— ❖ ————

*S*ummertime and lemonade go hand in hand and it's hard to imagine there was ever a time when you couldn't get it out of a can. If you've never tasted fresh lemonade, you should give it a try. The extra work is worth the experience. By the way, if you can't find any pink lemons, grenadine syrup works just as well.

2^1/2 cups superfine sugar
^{1}/2 cup grenadine syrup
3 cups freshly squeezed lemon juice
12 cups cold water

The best way to go about mixing beverages is to first make a syrup and then dilute it with larger quantities of water. (I save empty gallon bottles from bottled water for this purpose.) Begin by combining sugar, grenadine syrup, lemon juice, and 2 cups of water in a one gallon empty plastic bottle. Shake vigorously. Add 5 cups of water and shake again. Fill with remaining 5 cups of water. (Recipe may be doubled by repeating in a second bottle.)

PIG ROAST

❖

This once-Southern tradition has taken the rest of the country by storm. I was driving through Easton, Connecticut, of all places, when I saw a big cowboy-boot sign alongside the road. As I came closer to the sign, it read "PIG ROAST," with the spur pointing to a turn in the road. I wouldn't be at all surprised if they now have pig roasts in Alaska.

So what's all the fuss about? Pulled pork sandwiches. There are many interpretations of this classic. Generally Southerners cook the meat with a spicy mustard glaze. Texans and Midwesterners usually braise the pork in a smoky-sweet tomato barbecue sauce. As for Connecticut pig roasts . . . well, they sort of sit on the fence and serve it either way.

Pig Roast

❖

Pulled Pork Sandwiches
(Southern Style)

Pulled Pork Sandwiches
(Texas and Midwestern Style)

Cabbage and Corn Slaw

Picnic-style Potato Salad

Campfire Cake

Pulled Pork Sandwiches (Southern Style)
Makes 8 servings

❖

2 pounds pork shoulder, cut into large cubes
3 cups chopped onion
$1/4$ cup honey
$1/4$ cup molasses
1 to 2 teaspoons salt
1 teaspoon celery seed
1 teaspoon Worcestershire sauce
$1/4$ to $1/2$ teaspoon red pepper
$1/4$ cup yellow prepared mustard
$1/2$ cup cider vinegar
shredded lettuce
Bread-and-Butter Pickle Sauce
(recipe follows)
8 large sandwich rolls

Preheat oven to 325°F (170°C). Combine pork and onion in casserole. Blend honey, molasses, salt, celery seed, Worcestershire sauce, red pepper, mustard, and vinegar. Pour over pork and onions in casserole. Cover and bake until meat is very tender and breaks apart, $3^1/4$ to 4 hours. Shred meat with two forks and mix into sauce. Spoon into rolls. Top with shredded lettuce and more sauce.

Bread-and-Butter Pickle Sauce

1 cup mayonnaise
1 teaspoon paprika
$1/4$ cup minced bread-and-butter pickles
1 tablespoon pickle juice

Combine all ingredients in small bowl with wire whisk. Chill several hours to blend flavors.

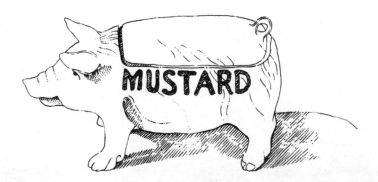

*Opposite: Cranberry Pumpkin Bread, page 54
and Shaker Sugar-Pumpkin Pie, page 56*

Pulled Pork Sandwiches (Texas and Midwestern Style)
Makes 8 Servings

❖

2 pounds pork shoulder, cut into large cubes
2 cups chopped onion
2 cups chopped green bell pepper
$1/2$ cup firmly packed light brown sugar
1 teaspoon dry mustard
1 tablespoon chili powder
$1/4$ cup red wine vinegar
2 teaspoons liquid smoke
6-ounce can tomato paste
$2/3$ cup apple juice
8 large sandwich rolls

Preheat oven to 325°F (170°C). Combine pork, onion, and bell pepper in 3-quart casserole. Blend brown sugar, mustard, chili powder, vinegar, liquid smoke, tomato paste, and apple juice and pour over meat mixture. Cover and bake until meat is very tender and breaks apart, $3^1/4$ to 4 hours. Shred meat with two forks and mix into sauce. Spoon into rolls and serve.

Opposite: Snowmen Meringues, page 58
and Gingerbread Teddy Bears, page 61

Cabbage and Corn Slaw
makes 8 servings

❖

Slaws and relishes are essential to any pig roast menu. Some feature cabbage, others feature corn, while this recipe is a marriage of both. Always make the salad a day in advance; it improves as it marinates.

6 cups shredded cabbage
2 cups cooked corn
$1/2$ cup diced red bell pepper
$1/2$ cup diced green bell pepper
$1/3$ cup sugar
$1/3$ cup distilled white vinegar
$2/3$ cup vegetable oil
1 teaspoon celery salt
$1/2$ teaspoon cracked black pepper
$1/2$ teaspoon dry mustard

Toss cabbage, corn, and peppers in large bowl. Blend sugar, vinegar, oil, celery salt, pepper, and dry mustard. Pour over cabbage mixture and toss. Cover and refrigerate several hours to blend flavors.

Picnic-style Potato Salad
makes 8 servings

❖

There are hundreds of potato salads made with wonderful imported mustards. But when it comes to picnic-style potato salad, call me nostalgic. I still make it the old-fashioned way, with yellow ballpark mustard.

1 1/2 pounds red-skinned potatoes
1/2 cup diced celery
1/2 cup diced, seeded cucumbers
1/2 cup sliced green onion
1 1/4 cups mayonnaise
1 tablespoon prepared mustard (ballpark style or spicy brown)
1 tablespoon sugar
1 tablespoon lemon juice
1/2 cup grated cheddar cheese
1 hard-cooked egg, chopped
1 teaspoon salt
1/2 teaspoon cracked black pepper

Cut small red potatoes in half, large ones in quarters. Place in large saucepan and cover with water. Bring to boil and cook until tender, about 15 to 20 minutes. Drain and chill. Toss potatoes in large bowl with celery, cucumber, and green onions. Blend mayonnaise, mustard, sugar, lemon juice, cheese, egg, salt, and pepper. Toss with potato mixture. Cover and chill at least 4 hours to blend flavors.

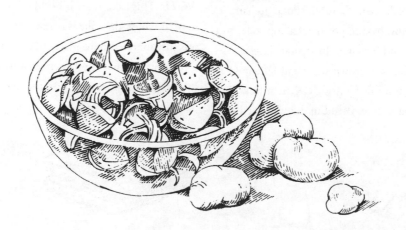

CAMPFIRE CAKE
MAKES ONE 13 × 9-INCH CAKE

❖

*R*emember the taste of S'mores? Can anything compare to those gooey, chocolate-covered graham crackers topped with fire-toasted marshmallows? This cake can. One bite will bring back childhood memories of that first camp out in the woods (or maybe it was the backyard?).

1 cup all-purpose flour
2 cups graham cracker crumbs
1 teaspoon baking powder
1/2 teaspoon baking soda
1/2 teaspoon salt
1 cup firmly packed light brown sugar
3/4 cup (1 1/2 sticks) unsalted butter, softened
3 eggs
1 cup milk
1 1/2 cups miniature semisweet chocolate chips
2 cups miniature marshmallows

Preheat oven to 350°F (180°C). Grease and flour 13 × 9-inch cake pan. Combine flour, graham cracker crumbs, baking powder, baking soda, and salt in bowl, and set aside. In separate large mixing bowl cream brown sugar and 1/2 cup (1 stick) butter until fluffy using electric mixer. Beat in eggs one at a time. Blend in dry ingredients and milk, then beat at medium speed 1 minute. Fold in 1 cup chocolate chips. Spread batter evenly in pan and bake until toothpick inserted in center comes out clean, 25 to 35 minutes. Cool 10 to 15 minutes. Meanwhile, melt remaining 1/2 cup chocolate chips and remaining 1/4 cup (1/2 stick) butter together. Blend until smooth and spread over top of cake. Scatter marshmallows over chocolate glaze. Place cake under broiler just until marshmallows are lightly browned and puffy. Swirl slightly with spatula.

NOTE: This cake is great hot! I've been to a pig roast at which the cake was too warm to slice; it was just spooned onto plates like a casserole. One way of achieving this effect is to bake the cake ahead of time, and broil the marshmallows just before serving.

CRAB CARNIVAL

❖

We were lost . . . somewhere between Washington, D.C., and Baltimore. Maybe we weren't anywhere near Baltimore. Miles back we had decided to take a detour to avoid all the weekend traffic. We were in rural Maryland and almost on empty—our gas tank and our stomachs. That's when we happened upon one of those delightful surprises in life: we stopped to fuel up at a crab carnival.

There were two tents; the first was filled with tables of people, hammers in hand, pounding away at hard-shell crabs. It looked like a lot of work for someone who was hungry and tired. I opted for the second tent. A more civilized meal was being served there, one of my favorites— Chesapeake crab cakes. The entire menu was memorable. Between the black-eyed pea salad and the spoon bread, I barely had room for dessert. But fortunately, I did save a little space. From a buffet of home-baked goodies I chose a slice of watermelon spice cake . . . worth every calorie.

CRAB CARNIVAL

❖

Chesapeake Crab Cakes With Cucumber Tartar Sauce

Black-Eyed Pea Salad

Potomac Spoon Bread

Watermelon Spice Cake With Buttermilk Sauce

Chesapeake Crab Cakes
MAKES 8 SERVINGS

❖

*O*ld Bay seasoning is the essential ingredient in just about every crab cake recipe ever created. It's possible to mix your own by combining ¹/4 teaspoon each celery salt and white pepper, and ¹/8 teaspoon each dry mustard, ground bay leaf, ground cardamom, mace, ginger, cinnamon, and paprika.

Authentic crab cakes are always panfried (never deep fried), but tastes and techniques vary. One method is to fill a skillet with 1 inch of cooking oil and heat it to 350°F (180°C). The crab cakes are fried until golden and crisp on each side. Sautéing them in a lightly oiled nonstick skillet, the more contemporary method, also produces a tasty crab cake, but the crust will not be as crisp nor will the edges of the cakes be browned.

2 pounds fresh lump crabmeat
3 tablespoons unsalted butter
¹/4 cup minced onion
¹/4 cup minced celery
¹/4 cup finely chopped green bell pepper
1 tablespoon Old Bay seasoning
¹/4 teaspoon salt
2 eggs or 3 egg whites
¹/2 cup mayonnaise
1 tablespoon chopped pimento
1 to 1¹/4 cups fresh bread crumbs
vegetable oil
CUCUMBER TARTAR SAUCE (recipe follows)

Pick over crabmeat, removing any pieces of shell. Melt butter in skillet over medium high heat. Add onion, celery, and bell pepper and sauté just until tender. Remove from heat and stir in crabmeat, Old Bay seasoning, and salt. Whisk eggs to blend in a separate mixing bowl. Blend in mayonnaise. Stir in crabmeat mixture, pimento, and enough bread crumbs to bind ingredients. Form mixture into 2¹/2-inch patties. (If frying crab cakes, coat with additional fresh bread crumbs. If you will be browning them in a nonstick pan, do not add breading.)

To Panfry

Heat 1 inch of vegetable oil in skillet to 350°F (180°C). Cook crab cakes on each side until crisp and golden brown. Remove with slotted spoon and drain on paper towels.

To Sauté

Coat a nonstick skillet with 2 to 4 tablespoons vegetable oil. Lightly brown crab cakes on both sides. Be sure they are heated through.

Serve either version with cucumber tartar sauce.

Cucumber Tartar Sauce

1 1/2 cups mayonnaise
1 tablespoon lemon juice
1 teaspoon dry mustard
1/2 teaspoon celery salt
1 tablespoon sugar
1 tablespoon minced fresh chives
2 tablespoons minced seeded cucumber
2 tablespoons minced
bread-and-butter pickles

Combine all ingredients in small bowl with wire whisk. Chill several hours to blend flavors.

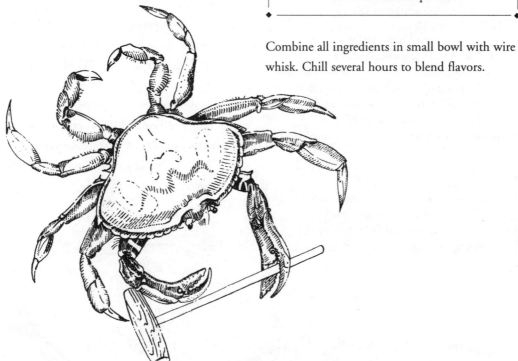

Black-Eyed Pea Salad
MAKES 8 SERVINGS

❖

Considered a Southern vegetable, black-eyed peas are often overlooked by the rest of the country. My mother is from Texas, and she insisted we eat them on New Year's Day for good luck.

2¹/2 cups water
1 teaspoon salt
two 10-ounce packages
frozen black-eyed peas
1 clove garlic, crushed
1 tablespoon firmly packed light brown sugar
1 tablespoon spicy brown mustard
3 tablespoons red wine vinegar
¹/2 cup peanut oil
10-ounce package frozen petite green peas,
thawed
2 ripe tomatoes, seeded and chopped
¹/2 cup diced celery
1 large green bell pepper, seeded and diced
¹/2 cup sliced green onion
¹/3 cup minced fresh parsley
¹/2 cup dry-roasted peanuts, chopped

Bring water to boil with salt in medium saucepan. Add black-eyed peas, cover, and simmer 30 minutes, or until tender. Make a paste of garlic, brown sugar, mustard, and vinegar in large mixing bowl. Whisk in oil a spoonful at a time until blended. Add green peas, tomatoes, celery, bell pepper, green onion, and parsley and toss with dressing. Drain beans well and toss with salad mixture. Cover and chill several hours to blend flavors. Toss with peanuts just before serving.

POTOMAC SPOON BREAD
MAKES 8 SERVINGS

❖

Throughout Maryland and Virginia spoon bread is served in place of bread, potatoes, or both. The dish dates back to colonial times, when it was considered a "convenience food." Spoon bread required no yeast, no rising, no kneading, and no rolling. Two centuries ago the eggs were whipped by hand—but you can cheat and use an electric mixer.

4 eggs
1/3 cup sugar
3/4 cup (1 1/2 sticks) unsalted butter
3 1/4 cups milk
1 teaspoon salt
2/3 cup + 1 tablespoon yellow cornmeal
1 cup cooked corn

Heat oven to 350°F (180°C). Grease 2-quart casserole. Combine eggs and sugar in large mixing bowl and beat with electric mixer on high speed until doubled in volume. Meanwhile, melt butter in large saucepan. Add milk and heat to just below boiling point; keep hot over very low heat. Add salt and gradually whisk in cornmeal; whisk constantly until mixture is very thick. Fold cornmeal mixture and corn into egg mixture with wire whisk. Pour into prepared casserole. Place casserole in shallow pan on oven rack; pour hot water around casserole to a depth of 1 inch. Bake until golden brown and a knife inserted in center comes out clean, about 1 1/4 hours. Serve hot.

WATERMELON SPICE CAKE
MAKES ONE 13 × 9-INCH CAKE

❖

This is one of those "magical mystery cakes" in the class of tomato soup cake, zucchini cake and, at one time, carrot cake (which is hardly mysterious anymore).

2 cups all-purpose flour
1 cup firmly packed light brown sugar
1 teaspoon baking soda
1 teaspoon salt
2 teaspoons cinnamon
1 teaspoon nutmeg
$^{1}/_{2}$ cup (1 stick) unsalted butter, softened
1 cup sour cream
2 eggs
1$^{1}/_{4}$ cups chopped watermelon pickle, well drained
BUTTERMILK SAUCE (recipe follows)

Preheat oven to 350°F (180°C). Grease and flour 13 × 9-inch pan. Combine flour, brown sugar, baking soda, salt, and spices in mixing bowl. Add butter, sour cream, and eggs and beat at medium speed 1 minute. Stir in watermelon pickles. Spread batter evenly in prepared pan.

Bake until toothpick inserted in center comes out clean, 30 to 38 minutes. Cut into squares and serve with buttermilk sauce.

BUTTERMILK SAUCE

1 cup sugar
2 tablespoons cornstarch
$^{1}/_{2}$ cup buttermilk
$^{1}/_{2}$ cup (1 stick) unsalted butter, cut into cubes
1 teaspoon vanilla

Combine sugar and cornstarch in saucepan. Blend in buttermilk. Stir in butter and bring sauce to boil, stirring constantly, until thickened and smooth. Remove from heat and stir in vanilla. Serve warm over warm cake.

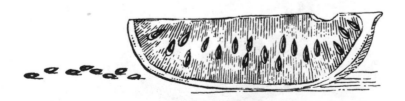

FIREHOUSE CHICKEN BARBECUE

❖

Every small town seems to have a charming firehouse with a volunteer fire department. They truly serve the community in every sense: If your cat gets stuck in a tree, they're there. If your dog falls into the Long Island Sound, they're there. If your poorly wired, turn-of-the-century house goes up in smoke, they're there!

On the Fourth of July they lead the parade down Main Street in their shiny new red (or yellow) trucks. And who doesn't look forward to the annual Firehouse Chicken Barbecue, complete with the antique fire engine and Dalmatians on display? This event always packs people in. After all, firefighters are as famed for their cooking as they are for putting out kitchen fires!

Firehouse Chicken Barbecue

❖

Honey-Glazed BBQ Chicken

Grilled Dill Toast

Apple Baked Beans

Green Rice Salad

Peaches and Cream Cobbler

Honey-Glazed BBQ Chicken
makes 8 servings

❖

*M*ost people make the mistake of basting their chicken too soon. Barbecue sauce burns long before the chicken begins to cook.

---

1 cup applewood chips
1/2 cup honey
6-ounce can orange juice concentrate
1/4 cup red wine vinegar
1 tablespoon whole mustard seed
1 bay leaf
1/2 cup ketchup
1/2 cup chili sauce
2 frying chickens, quartered
salt and pepper

Cover wood chips with water and let soak at least 1 hour. Bring honey, orange concentrate, vinegar, mustard seed, bay leaf, ketchup, and chili sauce to simmer in saucepan. Cover and simmer 20 minutes. Discard bay leaf.

Heat barbecue coals until glowing red. Set rack about 5 inches over coals. Sprinkle chicken parts with salt and pepper. Sear chicken over coals 5 minutes on each side. Drain wood chips and distribute evenly over coals, sprinkling them between spaces in the grill rack. Turn chicken bone side down. Cover, with vents partially closed, and smoke chicken 30 minutes. Remove cover and baste chicken with sauce. Cook until glazed, another 3 to 5 minutes on each side. Serve extra sauce on the side.

HELPFUL HINT: If you want to remove the skin from your chicken, do so just before basting with sauce. Keeping the skin on during the initial cooking will keep the chicken from drying out.

Opposite: Candy Cane Coffee Cakes With Fruit and Nut Filling and Almond Glaze, page 62

GRILLED DILL TOAST
MAKES 8 SLICES

❖

1/3 cup butter, softened
1 clove garlic, crushed
1 tablespoon snipped fresh dill or 1
teaspoon dried
eight 1-inch thick slices Italian or
French bread

Cream butter with garlic and dill. Spread on both sides of each bread slice. Grill about 5 inches above coals on barbecue until golden brown and toasted, about 1 minute on each side.

Opposite: Summer Bean Salad, page 78

Apple Baked Beans
makes 8 servings

❖

Always discard the soaking water from dried beans. This helps reduce the "gassy" feeling many people get from eating beans.

1¹/2 pounds (3 cups) pea beans
2 cups apple juice
1 teaspoon salt
1 large or 2 small ham hocks
1 large onion, thinly sliced
¹/2 cup firmly packed light or
dark brown sugar
¹/2 cup molasses
1 teaspoon dry mustard
¹/2 cup diced celery
3 cups firm, crisp apples, peeled,
cored and sliced

Soak beans in kettle of water overnight. Drain. Add apple juice, salt, ham hock, onion, and enough water to cover beans by 1 inch. Cover and simmer until beans are tender, about 2 hours. Remove ham hock. Cut meat away from bone and dice; return meat to beans and discard bone. Stir in all remaining ingredients and pour into 2-quart casserole.

Preheat oven to 300°F (150°C). Cover casserole and bake 3¹/2 hours. Remove cover and bake until beans are glazed on top, 30 to 45 more minutes.

GREEN RICE SALAD
MAKES 8 SERVINGS

❖

*G*reen rice, whether a hot casserole or a cold salad, is a classic Midwestern dish. Growing up, I can't remember a barbecue at which one version or the other wasn't served.

3 cups cooked white or brown rice
$1/2$ cup finely chopped celery
$1/2$ cup sliced green onion
$1/2$ cup minced fresh parsley
two 10-ounce packages frozen spinach, thawed and squeezed dry
2 cups lightly cooked, chopped broccoli
$3/4$ cup mayonnaise
$3/4$ cup buttermilk
1 tablespoon curry powder
1 teaspoon salt
1 teaspoon cracked pepper

Combine rice, celery, green onion, parsley, spinach, and broccoli in large mixing bowl and toss to combine. Blend mayonnaise with buttermilk until smooth and creamy. Season with curry powder, salt, and cracked pepper. Toss with rice mixture. Cover and chill several hours to blend flavors.

Peaches and Cream Cobbler
makes 9 servings

❖

The drop-style biscuit crust makes this cobbler particularly easy to make—no kneading or rolling involved.

1 cup plus 1 tablespoon sugar
3 tablespoons cornstarch
1/4 teaspoon nutmeg
1/2 teaspoon grated lemon peel
6 cups sliced peeled fresh peaches or nectarines
Cobbler Crust (recipe follows)
Cream Topping (recipe follows)

Preheat oven to 375°F (190°C). Combine 1 cup sugar, cornstarch, nutmeg, and lemon peel in 3-quart saucepan and cook, stirring with wooden spoon, until mixture thickens and boils. Pour into ungreased 8-inch square baking dish. Drop 9 equal spoonfuls of cobbler crust dough over peaches. Sprinkle remaining tablespoon sugar over dough. Bake until golden brown, 35 to 40 minutes. Serve warm with cream topping.

Cobbler Crust

1 cup all-purpose flour
1/4 cup sugar
2 teaspoon baking powder
1/4 cup (1/2 stick) unsalted butter
1/4 cup butter-flavored shortening
1/3 cup milk

Combine flour, sugar, and baking powder in mixing bowl. Cut in butter and shortening until mixture resembles fine crumbs. Stir in milk with fork, just until dough holds together.

Cream Topping

8-ounce package cream cheese, softened
1/4 cup superfine sugar
1 teaspoon vanilla
1/2 cup milk

Beat cream cheese, sugar, and vanilla together until smooth. Slowly blend in milk.

LOBSTER FEST

❖

Clambakes and lobster fests are a local tradition for many New England towns. I happen to live in a charming seaside Connecticut village where our lobster fest is a very big deal. Of course, there are probably a hundred others just like it going on up and down the shore. They frequently feature Yankee foods, such as brown bread and fiddleheads, when in season. However, all eyes and appetites are focused on the star attraction: LOBSTER! People stand in long lines just waiting for an empty chair at a long communal table; it's all part of the ritual. Watching others trying to dismantle their dinners with total abandon makes you want your own lobster even more. This is not a delicate meal. People dress very casually in shorts and T-shirts. When they leave, everyone knows where they've been—it's written all over their clothes.

Lobster Fest

❖

Boiled Lobster

Sweet Corn on the Cob

Dilled New Potatoes

Yankee Brown Bread

Fiddlehead Salad

Blueberry Ginger Cake With Lemon Sauce

New England Maple Walnut Pie

BOILED LOBSTER
ALLOW ONE 1¼- TO 2 LB-LOBSTER PER PERSON

❖

*B*oiling live lobster at home is very disturbing to some people. One minute the critter is crawling contentedly across the kitchen counter; the next minute it's struggling to stay out of boiling water. If you don't like the role of executioner, you're not alone. I'm not sure there's any humane way to kill anything, but I've been told that it's less cruel to first "tranquilize" your lobster. This is done by submerging it briefly in warm water in your sink. Apparently this puts it into a sleepy stupor and makes it safer to handle. By the way, always be sure to buy lobsters with pegged claws for your own protection.

---

1 tablespoon salt
1¼- to 2-pound lobster per person
lemon wedges
CLARIFIED BUTTER (recipe follows)

Fill very large pot or kettle with water. Add salt and bring to rolling boil. Cook lobsters no more than two at a time. Pick up lobster with tongs and plunge into water. Cover and simmer 5 minutes for the first pound of each lobster plus 3 minutes for each additional pound (e.g., two 2-pound lobsters should simmer 16 minutes). Remove lobsters from pot with tongs and drain. It's customary to crack through the length of the shell with a heavy knife or cleaver. (This makes lobster a little easier to handle.) Serve with lemon wedges and clarified butter. Provide a lobster cracker and pick for each person.

CLARIFIED BUTTER

Allow about 4 tablespoons butter per person. (This may sound indulgent, but people usually splurge when eating lobster.) Melt butter over low heat. Skim off foam with spoon and discard; strain clear yellow liquid through a fine sieve or cheesecloth. One cup butter yields about 13 tablespoons clarified butter.

SWEET CORN ON THE COB
ALLOW 1 TO 2 EARS PER PERSON

Sweet corn refers here to young, tender corn, freshly picked and served before it develops tough, starchy kernels. Some varieties are naturally sweeter than others. "Country Gentleman" is my favorite and the one I cultivate in my own backyard. "Silver Queen" and "Butter and Sugar" are also excellent. Whenever possible, avoid buying what our family refers to as "horse corn"—it's not really for livestock, but it might as well be. I once lost a filling on just such an ear of corn. Country cooks often sweeten the cooking water with sugar and milk before adding the corn. This seems to bring out the best in this summertime treat.

1 to 2 ears fresh corn per person
2 quarts water
1 cup whole milk
2 tablespoons sugar
2 teaspoons salt
CLARIFIED BUTTER (see page 108)

Remove husks and silk from corn. Combine water, milk, sugar, and salt in very large pot or kettle and bring to rolling boil. Add corn. When water returns to boil, cook 5 minutes; do not overcook. Serve with clarified butter.

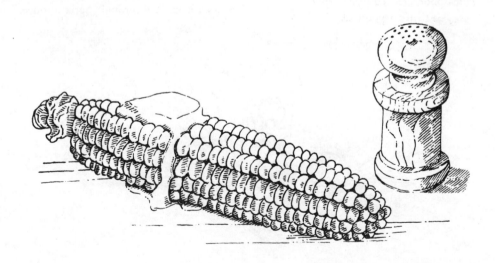

DILLED NEW POTATOES
MAKES 8 SERVINGS

❖

*I*n *New England any main course that's boiled in a pot will also be served with boiled new potatoes, seasoned with parsley and dill and tossed with butter or sour cream. With a buttery lobster dinner, I find buttered potatoes redundant. I prefer the sour cream version, and I've even tried using yogurt for half of the sour cream.*

2 pounds small red-skinned
potatoes, scrubbed
1 teaspoon salt
1 large red onion, thinly sliced
1 1/3 cups sour cream
or
2/3 cup sour cream and 2/3 cup
plain yogurt
1/3 cup chopped fresh dill
1/4 cup minced fresh parsley
1 teaspoon sugar
1/2 teaspoon cracked black pepper
1/2 to 1 teaspoon salt

Place potatoes in very large saucepan and cover with water. Add salt, bring to boil, and cook 15 minutes. Add onion and continue cooking until potatoes are tender but not falling apart, about 5 more minutes. Drain well. Keep potatoes warm in saucepan. Mix sour cream (or sour cream and yogurt) with dill, parsley, sugar, pepper, and salt in small bowl. Add to potatoes and gently toss. Warm over low heat so sour cream melts and potatoes are warmed through. Serve at once.

Yankee Brown Bread
MAKES TWO 1-POUND LOAVES

❖

It wouldn't be a New England meal without traditional brown bread. Alas, many people are intimidated by a brown bread recipe; there's a myth that it must be complicated because it's steamed, not baked. Nothing could be further from the truth. Brown bread is made with a simple quick-bread batter (no yeast to mix or rise). All you really need to worry about is saving two empty coffee cans.

1 cup wholewheat flour
1 cup sifted rye flour
1 cup white cornmeal
2 teaspoon baking soda
1 teaspoon salt
$1/2$ teaspoon nutmeg
2 cups buttermilk
$2/3$ cup molasses
1 cup raisins

Combine flours, cornmeal, baking soda, salt, and nutmeg in large mixing bowl. Blend buttermilk and molasses in large glass measuring cup. Pour into dry ingredients. Add raisins and stir just until ingredients are well moistened.

Grease two 1-pound cans (coffee cans hold 1 pound liquid measure, even though the coffee itself weighs 13 ounces). Divide batter between cans, filling about $2/3$ full. Grease two 12-inch squares of foil and cover open ends of cans, greased side down. Tie a length of string around can to secure foil.

Set up a steamer pot with a wire rack in the bottom, or improvise a steamer by placing 2 or 3 inverted custard cups on the bottom of a kettle and placing a wire rack on the cups. Set cans upright on rack and pour boiling water around cans to reach halfway up sides. Cover pot and steam bread 3 hours, adding water as needed to maintain same level. Bread is done when a long wooden skewer inserted through foil into center comes out clean. Remove cans from steamer and cool about 2 minutes, then immediately remove loaves from cans. Cool completely or chill before slicing. (Brown bread needs to "set"; it's best to reheat it rather than serve it straight from the steamer.)

FIDDLEHEAD SALAD
MAKES 8 SERVINGS

❖

Fiddlehead ferns are a rare find. They sprout up in parts of northern New England for a short time in May, although I've seen them in markets through mid-June. Finding fiddleheads holds the same mystique as hunting for morels or truffles—if you've found a place where they grow, you keep it a secret. Just ask anyone in that area . . . nobody will admit to knowing where they are! So what do you do when fiddlehead season is over? Well, you can freeze them, or you can make this salad with asparagus; the flavor is somewhat similar.

2 pounds very fresh fiddleheads (or asparagus*)
1/4 cup olive oil
3 cups sliced leeks, well washed
1 red bell pepper, cut into julienne
1 quart cherry tomatoes, halved
1/3 cup vegetable oil
2 tablespoons lemon juice
1 tablespoon red wine vinegar
1 teaspoon spicy brown mustard
1 teaspoon salt
1 teaspoon cracked black pepper
red-leaf lettuce

To "defuzz" fiddleheads, unwind each fern and wipe off brown fuzz with clean, damp cloth under cool running water. Place in large saucepan, cover with water, and bring to boil. Cook 8 minutes. Immediately remove fiddleheads with slotted spoon and plunge into cold water to stop cooking. Drain well in colander. Meanwhile, heat olive oil in medium skillet. Add leeks and bell pepper and sauté until crisp-tender, about 2 minutes. Transfer contents of skillet to large mixing bowl, and cool to room temperature. Add fiddleheads and cherry tomatoes. Blend vegetable oil, lemon juice, vinegar, mustard, salt and pepper in glass measuring cup and pour over vegetables; toss gently. Chill at least 3 hours to blend flavors. Serve salad over leaves of red-leaf lettuce.

NOTE: To substitute asparagus, first trim off tender tips, which are cooked last. Cut off tips diagonally, 2 inches from the end. Slice stalks diagonally at 2-inch intervals until you reach the tough bottom part; discard this. Keep tips separate from stalk pieces. Bring about 2 quarts water to rolling boil. Add stalk pieces and boil 2 to 3 minutes. Add tips and boil 1 minute longer. Immediately remove asparagus with slotted spoon and plunge into cold water to stop cooking. Drain well in colander. Add to leek mixture with cherry tomatoes and proceed as above.

HELPFUL HINT: I like to freeze fiddleheads for special meals throughout the year. Instead of cooking them for 8 minutes, just blanch them for about a minute in boiling water. Plunge them into cold water, drain well and pat dry. Arrange them on a tray lined with aluminum foil and freeze. After about 2 hours in the freezer, remove from foil and seal fiddleheads in a freezer bag. Reduce cooking time for frozen fiddleheads to about 5 minutes.

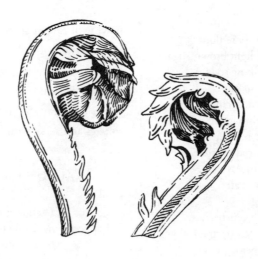

BLUEBERRY GINGER CAKE WITH LEMON SAUCE
MAKES ONE 9-INCH SQUARE CAKE

❖

Open any vintage New England cookbook and you'll find a dozen recipes for gingerbread. It was the standard cake of Yankee settlers, from fishermen to farmers. In the morning it was served with hot maple syrup; at supper it was a spicy bread to eat with a hearty stew. Variations evolved as colonial cooks got creative. Adding fruit, crumb toppings, or sauces elevated gingerbread to "ginger cake," and dessert status. I like this version because it has the best of everything: blueberries, a walnut crunch, and a tangy lemon sauce . . . the perfect way to finish a lobster fest!

2¹/₃ cups all-purpose flour
¹/₃ cup firmly packed light brown sugar
1 teaspoon baking soda
¹/₂ teaspoon salt
1 teaspoon ground ginger
1 teaspoon cinnamon
¹/₂ teaspoon nutmeg
¹/₂ cup butter-flavored shortening
1 cup light molasses
³/₄ cup hot water
1 egg
³/₄ to 1 cup fresh blueberries
WALNUT CRUMB TOPPING (recipe follows)
LEMON SAUCE (recipe follows)

Preheat oven to 325°F (170°C). Grease and flour 9-inch square pan, or line with baking parchment. Combine flour, brown sugar, baking soda, salt, and spices in mixing bowl. Add shortening, molasses, hot water, and egg, and beat at low speed of electric mixer for 30 seconds. Scrape bowl with rubber spatula and beat 1 minute longer. Fold in blueberries with spatula. Pour batter into prepared pan and sprinkle with topping. Bake until toothpick inserted in center comes out clean, 50 to 55 minutes. Cut into squares and serve with lemon sauce.

WALNUT CRUMB TOPPING

¹/₃ cup all-purpose flour
3 tablespoons firmly packed light brown sugar
¹/₄ teaspoon cinnamon
3 tablespoons chilled unsalted butter
¹/₄ cup chopped toasted walnuts*

Combine flour, brown sugar, and cinnamon in small bowl. Cut in butter until mixture is crumbly. Stir in walnuts.

NOTE: Toast walnuts in a 375°F (190°C) oven for 5 to 10 minutes, stirring 3 times while baking. Walnuts will continue to brown on top of gingerbread, so they should be only lightly toasted for this recipe.

LEMON SAUCE

¹/2 cup (1 stick) unsalted butter
1¹/3 cups sugar
2 eggs
¹/2 cup water
6 tablespoons fresh lemon juice
2 teaspoons grated lemon peel

Melt butter in medium saucepan. Remove from heat and stir in sugar. Beat eggs in small bowl with water, lemon juice, and peel. Pour egg mixture into butter mixture and cook over medium heat, whisking constantly, until sauce comes to boil and thickens. Serve warm over warm cake.

New England Maple Walnut Pie
MAKES ONE 9-INCH PIE

Yankees are very creative when it comes to using one of their greatest natural resources: maple syrup. From Vermont to Rhode Island it finds its way onto waffles and Johnny cakes and, of course, into dessert. This Northern version of pecan pie is every bit as simple to make and sinful to eat.

2 tablespoons unsalted butter
1 cup chopped walnuts
1/2 cup heavy cream
1 cup maple syrup
2/3 cup firmly packed light brown sugar
1/4 teaspoon salt
1 teaspoon vanilla
3 eggs
1 egg yolk
EGG AND VINEGAR PIE PASTRY
(single crust, page 8)

Preheat oven to 375°F (190°C). Heat butter in a medium-sized saucepan and sauté walnuts until golden. Remove pan from heat and stir in cream, maple syrup, brown sugar, salt, and vanilla. Beat eggs and egg yolk by hand in a medium-sized mixing bowl. Blend walnut mixture into beaten eggs. Pour into a pastry lined 9-inch pie plate (crimp edges of pastry as high as possible). Cover edges with strips of aluminum foil. Bake 30 minutes. Remove foil strips and continue baking until filling is set and pastry is golden, 15 to 20 minutes. Cool at least 2 hours before slicing.

Opposite: Strawberry Cream Biscuit Shortcakes, page 79

Opposite: Peaches and Cream Cobbler, page 104

CHURCH CHILI SUPPER

❖

Focal points of any community, from the elementary school to the town hall, sponsor chili suppers. They function as fund-raising events that are fun to attend. Chili suppers typically take place in dreary months.when there's not much else going on, making these welcome social gatherings.

In my experience, the worst chili suppers are held by schools and the best are held by churches. The schools utilized their own staff, ingredients, and recipe to serve . . . school chili! (Just what every kid wants for dinner after having it for lunch.) Churches took the potluck approach: volunteers donated everything from salad to dessert. I liked these chili suppers the best. There's a special spirit in teamwork that makes everything seem to taste better.

Church Chili Supper

❖

Three-Bean Oven-Baked Chili

Indian Creek Salad

Confetti Cornbread

Apple Brown Betty With Cinnamon Sauce

Frozen Peanut Butter Pie

THREE-BEAN OVEN-BAKED CHILI
MAKES 8 SERVINGS

— ❖ —

I've been to many chili suppers in my life, and I've learned one thing: this is not a good time to worry about which volunteers did or didn't soak the beans overnight. Even though the same recipe was passed out to everyone, I've managed to ladle up a bowl as hard as buckshot! The solution is standardization. I always suggest a simple-to-follow recipe using canned beans, with frozen limas for accent. The best part is that it's baked in the oven—no more tossing out pots of scorched chili from the cooks who got tired of watching (and stirring) it on the stove. This chunky, fork-style chili is easy for everyone to bake and bring in a casserole dish.

2 pounds ground beef
1 cup chopped onion
1 red bell pepper, chopped
1 green bell pepper, chopped
1/2 cup diced celery
2 tablespoons chili powder
1 teaspoon garlic powder
1 teaspoon cumin
1 teaspoon dried oregano
1 teaspoon cocoa
1 teaspoon salt
1/2 teaspoon dry mustard
1 tablespoon Worcestershire sauce
2 drops hot pepper sauce
15 1/2-ounce can stewed tomatoes
15 1/2-ounce can red kidney beans, drained
15 1/2-ounce can pinto beans, drained
9-ounce package frozen baby lima beans, thawed
1 cup ketchup
1/4 cup firmly packed dark brown sugar
2 tablespoons honey
1 tablespoon red wine vinegar

Preheat oven to 350°F (180°C). In large skillet brown ground beef with onion, peppers, and celery. Drain off as much fat as possible. Stir in chili powder, garlic powder, cumin, oregano, cocoa, salt, dry mustard, Worcestershire sauce, and pepper sauce and heat through, coating meat with spices. Stir in tomatoes, beans, ketchup, brown sugar, honey, and vinegar. Pour into 4-quart casserole. Cover and bake 25 minutes. Uncover and bake 20 minutes longer. Serve hot with warm cornbread. The flavor of this chili improves when the mixture is prepared in advance and refrigerated overnight.

INDIAN CREEK SALAD
MAKES 8 SERVINGS

❖

When I was growing up in Kansas City, there was a wonderful restaurant on the outskirts of town called Indian Creek Inn. It was famous for its country dinners and house dressing—a buttermilk recipe, long before the words "ranch dressing" had swept the country and become part of the common vocabulary. I remember waiting hours for a table and memorizing all of the copper gelatin molds that decorated the walls. The salad had a cult following, and everyone tried to copy it. Clones showed up at all the local chili suppers.

What ever happened to Indian Creek Inn? Like so much of our country, it went the way of "progress." Bulldozers and shopping mall developers destroyed Indian Creek and the inn. All that's left is the salad dressing.

---

6 cups packed fresh spinach
3 cups torn red-leaf lettuce
3 cups torn Boston lettuce
1 cup thinly sliced button mushrooms
1 cup grated white cheddar cheese
INDIAN CREEK DRESSING (recipe follows)

---

1 1/2 cups mayonnaise
1 cup buttermilk
2 tablespoons onion juice
2 tablespoons minced dill pickle
2 tablespoons minced fresh parsley
2 tablespoons minced fresh chives
1 tablespoon sugar
2 teaspoons whole mustard seed
1/2 teaspoon celery seed
1 teaspoon salt
1/2 to 1 teaspoon cracked black pepper

Combine thoroughly washed and dried greens in a very large salad bowl. Chill. Just before serving, toss with mushrooms and cheese. Serve with Indian Creek dressing.

INDIAN CREEK DRESSING

Do not try to mix this dressing in the blender. It will break down and become very thin.

Combine all ingredients in medium bowl and whisk until smooth. Transfer to glass jar and chill at least 8 hours to blend flavors.

CONFETTI CORNBREAD
MAKES 8 TO 9 SERVINGS

❖

*I*t's hard to imagine a chili supper without cornbread. This one's spiked with green onion, bell
peppers, and kernels of corn. Before you reach for a can, try cutting some corn fresh off the cob.
When corn is in season, I often wrap the ears in plastic, pop them in the microwave for a few
minutes, and keep them wrapped in the refrigerator, waiting for use in salads, soups, and, of
course, cornbread.

1¹/₂ cups all-purpose flour
¹/₂ cup yellow cornmeal
1 tablespoon baking powder
1 teaspoon salt
¹/₂ teaspoon dry mustard
3 eggs
¹/₂ cup milk
3 tablespoons honey
¹/₃ cup unsalted butter, melted
¹/₄ cup finely chopped red bell pepper
¹/₄ cup finely chopped green bell pepper
¹/₄ cup finely chopped green onion
1 cup cooked fresh or frozen corn

Combine flour, cornmeal, baking powder, salt, and dry mustard in medium bowl. Beat eggs in separate bowl or glass measure. Blend in milk, honey, and melted butter. Add egg mixture to dry ingredients along with peppers, green onions, and corn and gently fold together with rubber spatula until all ingredients are evenly moistened. Spread batter in prepared pan and bake until toothpick inserted in center comes out clean, 25 to 30 minutes. Serve warm.

Preheat oven to 425°F (250°C). Grease 9-inch square pan or line with baking parchment.

Apple Brown Betty With Cinnamon Sauce
makes 9 servings

❖

B*rown Betty differs from apple crisp in that the topping is made from some type of crumbs as opposed to flour. I prefer graham cracker crumbs to bread crumbs.*

6 cups thinly sliced firm, crisp apples
1/2 cup raisins
1/2 cup orange juice
1 tablespoon lemon juice
1 cup graham cracker crumbs
1/2 cup firmly packed light brown sugar
1 teaspoon cinnamon
1/4 teaspoon nutmeg
6 tablespoons (3/4 stick) unsalted butter, melted
Cinnamon Sauce (recipe follows)

Cinnamon Sauce

1 pint chilled heavy cream
1/3 cup firmly packed light brown sugar
1 teaspoon cinnamon
1 teaspoon vanilla

Combine cream, brown sugar, cinnamon, and vanilla in large bowl and whip just until soft peaks begin to form. Serve chilled.

Preheat oven to 350°F (180°C). Spray 9-inch square pan with nonstick cooking spray. Layer apples in pan; sprinkle evenly with raisins. Blend orange and lemon juices in small glass measure and pour over apples. Combine graham cracker crumbs, brown sugar, and spices in small bowl, and stir in melted butter. Sprinkle crumb mixture over apples. Bake until apples are tender and topping is crisp, 50 to 55 minutes. Serve warm with chilled cinnamon sauce.

FROZEN PEANUT BUTTER PIE
MAKES ONE 9-INCH PIE

❖

During the late sixties "grasshopper pie" swept the country by storm, soon to be followed by the next wave of "mud pie." These desserts were based on the same theme: a simple frozen mousse-like concoction in a chocolate cookie crust. By the seventies peanut butter pie was new to the scene and showing up at chili suppers all over town. It's still my favorite of the entire genre, and one of my fondest comfort foods.

8-ounce package cream cheese, softened
$1/3$ cup creamy peanut butter
$2/3$ cup firmly packed light brown sugar
1 teaspoon vanilla
1 pint chilled heavy cream
9-inch CHOCOLATE COOKIE CRUST
(recipe follows)
$1/3$ cup chopped roasted peanuts (unsalted)
PEANUT BUTTER FUDGE SAUCE
(recipe follows)

Combine cream cheese, peanut butter, brown sugar, and vanilla in a large mixing bowl. Beat until light and fluffy. Blend in $1/3$ cup of the heavy cream and beat until smooth. Set peanut butter mixture aside and whip remaining cream in a separate bowl until stiff. Gently fold whipped cream into peanut butter mixture. Pile into pie crust and sprinkle top with peanuts. Freeze until firm. Slice and serve with fudge sauce.

CHOCOLATE COOKIE CRUST

$1^1/2$ cups crushed chocolate wafer crumbs
$1/4$ cup ($1/2$ stick) unsalted butter, melted

Preheat oven to 350°F (180°C). Combine chocolate wafer crumbs and butter in a medium-sized mixing bowl. Press against the bottom and sides of a 9-inch pie plate and bake for 6 minutes. Chill crust before filling.

PEANUT BUTTER FUDGE SAUCE

16-ounce can of chocolate syrup
$1/4$ cup peanut butter
2 tablespoons unsalted butter

Combine chocolate syrup, peanut butter, and butter in a small saucepan. Cook over low heat, stirring until smooth.

PANCAKE BREAKFAST

❖

Pancake breakfasts are very popular in both spring and fall. These all-day brunch events frequently last well into the afternoon. On Shrove Tuesday, before Lent, many churches sponsor pancake suppers; the menu is pretty much the same for a day or evening meal. Usually there's a choice of two types of pancakes, with various syrups and toppings, and two breakfast meats. Fruit salad is often served, along with coffee and juice.

I remember helping my mother in the kitchen at my first pancake breakfast. I must have been barely five years old. Pancakes were flipping in the air everywhere as volunteers tried to feed a line of hungry people holding plates. I took great delight in retrieving the ones that fell to the floor, even though I was forbidden to eat them.

Pancake Breakfast

❖

Ginger-Apple Pancakes With Cider Syrup and
Pecan Butter

Blueberry Corn Cakes With Orange-Maple Sauce and
Orange "Chutter"

Breakfast Fruit Salad

Oven-Baked Bacon and Glazed Canadian Bacon

GINGER-APPLE PANCAKES WITH CIDER SYRUP AND PECAN BUTTER
MAKES EIGHT 4-INCH PANCAKES

❖

Fresh apples are baked into these pancakes while they're cooking on the griddle. For this reason, it's important to slice the apples very thin. When paired with cider syrup and pecan butter, they are simply irresistible.

1 egg
1/3 cup apple juice
1/2 cup buttermilk
2 tablespoons firmly packed dark brown sugar
1 tablespoon light molasses
2 tablespoons unsalted butter, melted
1 tablespoon vegetable oil
1 cup wholewheat flour
1 teaspoon baking powder
1/2 teaspoon baking soda
1/4 teaspoon salt
1/2 teaspoon cinnamon
1/2 teaspoon ginger
1/4 teaspoon nutmeg
2 crisp apples
1 tablespoon lemon juice
1 tablespoons granulated sugar
unsalted butter or butter-flavored shortening for griddle
CIDER SYRUP (recipe follows)
PECAN BUTTER (recipe follows)

Beat egg in large mixing bowl with wire whisk or electric mixer until light and frothy. Slowly beat in apple juice, buttermilk, brown sugar, molasses, butter, and oil. Combine flour, baking powder, baking soda, salt, and spices in separate bowl. Add dry ingredients to liquid ingredients, blending by hand with wire whisk or rubber spatula just until batter is smooth; do not overmix. Halve and core apples, but do not peel. Cut into 1/8-inch thick slices. Mix lemon juice and sugar in bowl, add apple slices and toss to coat (this will prevent browning). Have apples ready while cooking pancakes.

Heat griddle or skillet to about 375°F (190°C); droplets of water will "dance" on griddle when it has reached the right temperature. Lightly grease griddle. For each pancake, ladle 1/4 cup batter onto griddle. Spread about 4 apple slices across each pancake. As soon as pancakes are puffed and look dry around the edges, gently turn with spatula and cook other side until golden brown. Serve hot with warm cider syrup and scoops of pecan butter.

Cider Syrup

1/2 cup sugar
4 teaspoons cornstarch
1/4 teaspoon cinnamon
1 cup apple juice
1/4 cup honey

Combine sugar, cornstarch, and cinnamon in medium saucepan. Whisk in apple juice and cook over medium heat, stirring constantly, until slightly thickened. Remove from heat and stir in honey.

Pecan Butter

1/2 cup (1 stick) unsalted butter, softened
2 tablespoons powdered sugar
1/2 teaspoon vanilla
1/3 cup chopped toasted pecans, cooled*

Cream butter with powdered sugar until light and fluffy. Blend in vanilla and pecans.

*NOTE: Toast pecans in a 375°F (190°C) oven for 5 to 10 minutes, stirring 3 times while baking.

Blueberry Corn Cakes
Makes Eight 4-inch Pancakes

❖

Cornmeal pancakes are particularly popular in the New England states, where they're often combined with fresh blueberries. The berries are added at the last minute so they're less likely to turn the batter purple. Serve with orange-maple sauce and orange "chutter" (a cream cheese and butter spread).

1 egg
1 cup buttermilk
1 tablespoon sugar
1 tablespoon butter, melted
1 tablespoon vegetable oil
1 teaspoon grated orange peel
1/2 cup all-purpose flour
1/2 cup cornmeal
1 teaspoon baking powder
1/2 teaspoon baking soda
1/4 teaspoon salt
1/4 teaspoon nutmeg
3/4 cup fresh blueberries
unsalted butter or butter-flavored
shortening for griddle
ORANGE-MAPLE SAUCE (recipe follows)
ORANGE "CHUTTER" (recipe follows)

Beat egg in large mixing bowl with wire whisk or electric mixer until light and frothy. Slowly beat in buttermilk, sugar, butter, oil, and orange peel. Combine flour, cornmeal, baking powder, baking soda, salt, and nutmeg in separate bowl. Stir dry ingredients into liquid ingredients with wire whisk or rubber spatula just until smooth; do not overmix. Fold in blueberries just before cooking.

Heat griddle or skillet to about 375°F (190°C); droplets of water will "dance" on griddle when it has reached the right temperature. Lightly grease griddle. For each pancake, ladle 1/4 cup batter onto griddle. As soon as pancakes are puffed and look dry around the edges, gently turn with spatula and cook other side until golden brown. Serve hot with warm orange-maple sauce and orange "chutter."

ORANGE-MAPLE SAUCE

2 tablespoons unsalted butter
2 tablespoons all-purpose flour
$1/2$ cup orange juice
1 teaspoon grated orange peel
1 cup maple syrup

Melt butter in medium saucepan over medium low heat. Blend in flour, stirring until smooth and bubbly. Blend in orange juice and peel and cook, stirring constantly, until smooth and thickened. Blend in maple syrup and heat through.

ORANGE "CHUTTER"

$1/3$ cup unsalted butter, softened
3-ounce package cream cheese, softened
1 tablespoon orange juice concentrate, thawed
1 teaspoon grated orange peel

Cream butter and cream cheese in mixing bowl until light and fluffy. Blend in orange juice concentrate and orange peel.

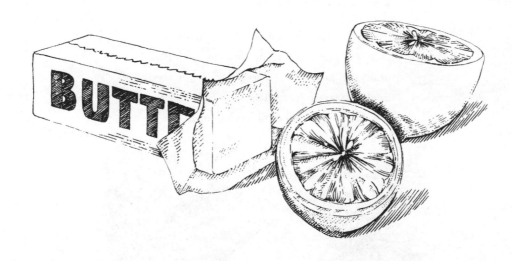

Breakfast Fruit Salad
makes 8 servings

❖

*G*inger poppy seed dressing contains lime juice, which helps keep the fruit looking fresh, even when it has to sit out for several hours.

1 pint strawberries, halved
1 pint blueberries
1 cup seedless grapes
1 cup honeydew melon balls
1 cup cantaloupe melon balls
1 cup fresh pineapple chunks
3 tablespoons fresh lime juice
1/4 cup honey
1 teaspoon poppy seeds
2 tablespoons finely chopped candied ginger

Combine strawberries, blueberries, grapes, melon balls, and pineapple in large mixing bowl. Blend lime juice, honey, poppy seed, and ginger together in glass measuring cup. Pour over fruit and gently toss. Cover and chill until serving time.

Opposite: Confetti Corn Bread, page 122

OVEN-BAKED BACON AND GLAZED CANADIAN BACON
MAKES 8 SERVINGS

———— ✦ ————

M*ost community cooking facilities, such as schools, churches, and firehouses, have limited rangetop space. Pancake breakfasts or suppers are like short-order cooking for a crowd; just making the pancakes usually takes up the entire stove. For this reason, bacon is almost always baked in the oven. Allow 3 to 4 ounces uncooked bacon per person.*

OVEN-BAKED BACON

Preheat oven to 400°F (200°C). Separate strips of 2 pounds bacon and stretch across rack in broiler pan. Bake until brown and as crisp as desired, 10 to 13 minutes. Drain on paper towels and keep warm.

GLAZED CANADIAN BACON

Preheat oven to 325°F (170°C). Place 2-pound roll of Canadian bacon in shallow roasting pan. Combine 1 tablespoon orange juice concentrate and 1 tablespoon honey. Brush over roll and bake until glazed, 20 to 30 minutes. Slice 1/4 inch thick.

Opposite: Pancake Breakfast, page 126

BAKING MEASUREMENTS

❖

Here are some general kitchen measurements which may be of help in your baking. These measurements are for U.S. cooks.

3 teaspoons = 1 tablespoon
4 tablespoons = $1/4$ cup
$5^1/3$ tablespoons = $1/3$ cup
8 tablespoons = $1/2$ cup

1 cup = $1/2$ pint or 8 fluid ounces
2 cups = 1 pint or 16 fluid ounces
1 quart (liquid) = 2 pints or 4 cups
1 gallon (liquid) = 4 quarts

5 whole eggs = 1 cup
8 to 10 egg whites = 1 cup
10 to 12 egg yolks = 1 cup

8 tablespoons butter = $1/2$ cup or 1 stick
2 sticks butter = 1 cup
2 cups butter = 1 pound

3 packages active dry yeast = 1 cake yeast
1 package active dry yeast = 1 scant tablespoon

1 square chocolate = 1 ounce or 1 tablespoon melted
1 ounce unsweetened chocolate = $1/3$ cup cocoa powder

1 pound apples = 3 cups peeled, cored, and sliced
6 ounces raisins = 1 cup
$1/4$ pound walnuts will yield 1 cup shelled
1 pound walnuts will yield $1/2$ pound shelled

1 lemon yields $2^1/2$ to $3^1/2$ tablespoons juice
1 orange yields 5 to 6 tablespoons juice

12 ounces honey = 1 cup
1 pound confectioners' sugar = $3^1/2$ cups
1 pound brown sugar = $2^1/4$ cups
1 pound granulated sugar = 2 cups

1 pound flour = approximately 4 cups
1 pound cake flour = $4^1/2$ cups
1 pound whole wheat flour = $3^3/4$ cups

Conversion Tables

❖

Outside the U.S., cooks measure more items by weight. Here are approximate equivalents for basic items in this book.

	U.S. Customary	Metric	Imperial
Apples (peeled and chopped)	2 cups	225 g	8 ounces
Butter	1 cup	225 g	8 ounces
	$1/2$ cup	115 g	4 ounces
	$1/4$ cup	60 g	2 ounces
	1 tablespoon	15 g	$1/2$ ounce
Chocolate chips	$1/2$ cup	85 g	3 ounces
Coconut (shredded)	$1/2$ cup	60 g	2 ounces
Flour (all purpose)	1 cup	150 g	5 ounces
Fruit (chopped)	1 cup	225 g	8 ounces
Nut Meals (chopped)	1 cup	115 g	4 ounces
Raisins (and other dried fruits)	1 cup	175 g	6 ounces
Sugar (granulated) or	1 cup	190 g	$6 1/2$ ounces
	$1/2$ cup	85 g	3 ounces
	$1/4$ cup	40 g	$1 3/4$ ounces
caster (confectioners')	1 cup	80 g	$2 2/3$ ounces
or icing	$1/2$ cup	40 g	$1 1/3$ ounces
	$1/4$ cup	20 g	$3/4$ ounce
brown	1 cup	160 g	$5 1/3$ ounces

Oven Temperatures

Fahrenheit	225	300	350	400	450
Celsius	110	150	180	200	230
Gas Mark	$1/4$	2	4	6	8

Emergency Substitutions

❖

If You Don't Have	Substitute
1 cup cake flour	1 cup minus 2 tablespoons all-purpose flour
1 tablespoon cornstarch (for thickening)	2 tablespoons all-purpose flour
1 teaspoon baking powder	$1/4$ teaspoon baking soda plus $1/2$ cup buttermilk or sour milk (to replace $1/2$ cup of the liquid called for in the recipe)
1 package active dry yeast	1 cake compressed yeast
1 cup granulated sugar	1 cup packed brown sugar or 2 cups sifted powdered sugar
1 cup honey	$1 1/4$ cups granulated sugar plus $1/2$ cup water
1 square (1 ounce) unsweetened chocolate	3 tablespoons unsweetened cocoa powder plus 1 tablespoon margarine or butter
1 cup buttermilk	1 tablespoon lemon juice or vinegar plus whole milk to make 1 cup. Let stand 5 minutes before using.
1 cup whole milk	$1/2$ cup evaporated milk plus $1/2$ cup water or 1 cup reconstituted nonfat dry milk plus $2 1/2$ teaspoons margarine or butter
1 cup half-and-half	1 cup minus 2 tablespoons whole milk plus 2 tablespoons margarine or butter
1 teaspoon finely grated lemon peel	$1/2$ teaspoon lemon extract

Index

———— ❖ ————